CW00404690

A Respectable Life

Leeds in the 1930s

by

Eric M. Sigsworth

Foreword

by

Richard Hoggart

Highgate of Beverley

Highgate Press (Markham) Limited
1995

EDITOR'S ACKNOWLEDGEMENTS

Grateful acknowledgements are due to the following who contributed in various ways to the publication of this volume:

To the University of Humberside for a generous contribution to the cost of publication;

To Leeds Leisure Services for permission to reproduce photographs from the Local History Collection;

To *The Yorkshire Evening Post* for permission to reproduce photographs from its photographic archives;

To Louis Billington, University of Hull, for reading the proof copy with an historical eye and helping me to appreciate these reminiscences as part of a genre.

To John Markham of Highgate Press who has given such enthusiastic and knowledgeable help at the publication stage;

And finally to Barry Sage of BA Print for his good humoured advice on converting print on disc and other technicalities.

British Library Cataloguing in Publication Data.
A catalogue record for this book is available from the British Library.

© 1994 Sheelagh Strawbridge

ISBN 1 899498 01 X

Published by

Highgate of Beverley
Highgate Press (Markham) Limited
24 Wylies Road, Beverley, HU17 7AP
Telephone (01482) 866826

Produced by

4 Newbegin, Lairgate, Beverley, HU17 8EG
Telephone (01482) 886017

Cover Picture: Leeds City Tram (by courtesy of Leeds Leisure Services) and the author as a boy.

Contents

List of Illustrations

Editor's Note

Eric Sigsworth completed a typescript he called *Number 5 Tram* not long before his totally disabling illness made it impossible for him to continue this work. Although he was too ill to discuss the manuscript in detail he agreed that I should edit it for publication. After his death, in 1992, it seemed appropriate that a social historian should provide a preface and further editorial expertise for Eric's final work.

Jim Leonard, who was a friend and colleague of Eric, has done more than this. He has put these reminiscences clearly in the context of Eric Sigsworth's work as an historian and has helped us to understand and appreciate some of the development and evolution of Eric's writing, with his reminiscences a most suitable culmination. Reading Jim Leonard's preface we are reminded that historians cannot pursue their work in a social and political vacuum and that writing history is a social and political activity. Those of us who encountered Eric Sigsworth towards the close of his professional life will remember his ability to to make accessible both pathetic and humorous aspects of nineteenth-century history and show their relevance to our contemporary concerns. These reminiscences, too, have this capacity for speaking to us directly, while retaining some of the social historian's analytical detachment.

In his preface Jim Leonard tells us that he has similar roots to Eric, in working-class Leeds, and Jim's personal understanding of these reminiscences gives an added dimension to our understanding of them. But it says much for the authenticity and relevance of Eric Sigsworth's final work that it speaks too to someone like myself, of different social class and geographical origins and of a different generation and gender. To those of us who were Second World War babies, Eric writes of the world of our parents, particularly the world of a young boy growing up, and it is this aspect of the reminiscences which speaks to *me* most directly.

Given the way in which this history was written, inevitably there is some overlapping of material. Jim Leonard has given titles to Eric's chapters which recognise the discrete nature of most of these, while leaving intact those which are rather a 'mixed bag'. I have not re-arranged Eric's text except in the few places where this was absolutely necessary for clarity and continuity: the language and style remain his. No attempt has been made to verify details, historical or geographical: these have been left as the author remembered them. I have added an occasional explanation [in square brackets] where a colloquial word might be puzzling to readers. Jim

Leonard has provided a bibliographical note for those readers who wish to look further into the context and framework.

As Jim Leonard has remarked, these reminiscences are the most personal of Eric's work and it seems appropriate to conclude this Note in a personal way. In writing it, I am struck by how fitting it seems that Eric's final work should be seen to the publication stage by a colleague whom he encouraged to publish, as, throughout his career, he encouraged many other colleagues, friends and research students. It is fitting, too, that Sheelagh Strawbridge, Eric's second wife, and his son, Michael, were my companions in Leeds for a day to choose photographs for the book. Michael showed me part of Leeds through a native historian's eyes, prefacing some of his commentary with things his father had told him about the city's history. I feel certain that his involvement in this project would have pleased Eric

Finally, I feel certain, too, that Eric would have wanted an acknowledgement of the support given to him in his last venture by his wife and by his mother-in-law, Ethel Strawbridge. It was at Sheelagh's insistence that Eric reluctantly learned to use a word-processor when he could no longer write by hand, and Ethel incorporated into her already-full carer's role the job of sorting out some of his word-processing muddles. Without Sheelagh and Ethel he could not have turned his handwritten manuscript into the typescript which we have prepared for publication. Although Eric could no longer physically speak by the time he died, this volume is essentially his authentic voice.

Rosamund Billington
School of Social Sciences and Professional Studies
University of Humberside
September, 1994

Tram shelter, Briggate

By courtesy of Leeds Leisure Services

Foreword

by

Richard Hoggart

I don't really imagine that Leeds produces more writers to celebrate its character than, say, Manchester or Birmingham. But to the natives it sometimes seems like that. In this generation alone one easily thinks of Keith Waterhouse, Willis Hall, Alan Bennett, Tony Harrison and, now, Eric Sigsworth.

The place does seem to have an unusual, noisy, colourful life. The only town I have lived in which had that sort of vitality is Naples; and that comparison, far-fetched though it appears at first, is apt. The dominant street music of Naples is the crying of hawkers, that of Leeds the squeal and rattle of trams. Or was. But here again in this generation both Alan Bennett and Eric Sigsworth remember those trams, the gondolas of the poor.

Eric Sigsworth responds very well indeed to the 'thisness', the texture, the detail piled on pile of the place. He has that essential ability: virtually total recall. In addition to this natural skill, each writer of this kind must have at least one other sense fully at work: such as smell, hearing, sight. In this memoir the most striking and evocative senses at work are the ear for local idiom and curious custom. Look at the chapter on seaside boarding-houses, especially on the mixture of prison-camp rules and adaptability towards that odd tribe, the 'self-caterers'; or the tenacious puritanical, secure home-keeping neurosis of those streets.

There is, though, an overall charity here, a charity some of us would have found hard to exercise so well; as in the description of the odious Leeds Grammar School of those days. What its manner is like now I do not know; but Tony Harrison, a decade after Eric Sigsworth, also recalls its insistent provincial snobberies. Not the Leeds most of us want to remember. But, as I say, Eric Sigsworth shows more charity there than some of us could muster.

Perhaps that charity was born out of another characteristic of those huddled districts, family love. Here again one recalls those other writers about Leeds; an all-embracing family was so often the key to, the origin of, their love of the place. Much of the poverty of those times has gone, thank God; it is doubtful whether the homeliness, the home-making, and the neighbourliness, so devotedly described here, have altogether disappeared.

Bibliographical Note

There is plenty of material on Leeds for the whole of that city's history. Restricting ourselves to the 1930s, if one wants to match the immediacy of Eric's style, then contemporary documents and press coverage must be referred to. This would entail visits to the Local History Department of Leeds Reference Library, and to the Archives collection in Sheepscarr.

Useful accounts of Leeds at this time can be had from F.J. Fowler's contribution, 'Urban Renewal 1918-39', in M.W. Beresford and G.R. Jones (eds) *Leeds and Its Region* (1967); and M. Meadowcroft's piece, 'The Years of Political Transition 1914-39', in D. Fraser (ed) *The History of Modern Leeds* (1980). Similarly, there is some interesting material in M.S. Gibson and M.J. Langstaff, *An Introduction to Urban Renewal* (1982).

For those who would prefer the more pictorial or perambulatory approach there are some worthwhile accounts: N. Pevsner, *Buildings of England: Yorkshire West Riding*, 2nd ed. (1967); D. Lindstrum, *Historic Architecture of Leeds* (1969); I.E. Broadhead, *Exploring Leeds* (1981); P. Nuttgens and A. Rutherford, *Leeds, Old and New* (1976) includes some photographs of trams in the same streets that Eric mentions.

For those who would like to explore attitudes to and changes in Leeds housing at this time there is much to go on, such as City of Leeds, *A Short History of Civic Housing* (1954); M.W. Beresford, 'The Back to Back House in Leeds 1787-1937', in J. Melling (ed) *Housing, Social Policy and the State* (1980). Maurice Beresford's, 'The Urban Garden in Leeds', in Philip Swan and David Foster (eds) *Essays in Regional and Local History* (Hutton Press, 1992) adds an interesting dimension to the houses described by Eric Sigsworth. Finally, as one would expect in regard to the 'back-to-back capital of the world', there are a number of unpublished theses such as G.W. Rhodes, *Housing Development in Leeds* 1919-39, Leeds University M.A., 1954, and R. Finnegan, *Housing Policy in Leeds*, 1918-39, Bradford University M.Phil., 1981.

Preface

In many ways this book is the lightest of Eric Sigsworth's voluminous work. It is certainly the most personal. Whilst his recently published biography of Montague Burton* must be seen as Eric's last major piece of published scholarship, it is not inappropriate that this present volume, published posthumously, is his last piece of completed work.

Eric's notable academic career spanned forty years, and was recently commemorated in *Essays in Regional and Local History*, edited by Philip Swan and David Foster. His first book, *Black Dyke Mills*, published in 1958, was a re-working of his doctoral thesis, and this particular avenue of enquiry led Eric to describe himself as a textile historian. From this area of expertise he moved into many related aspects of nineteenth- and twentieth-century social and economic history, including housing, demography, prostitution, business, and brewing; he became, in fact, a social historian in the very widest sense.

Viewed from one perspective, Eric's career did a full circle: the Burton book returned to the theme of textile history, albeit in a much more personal way than that of his first venture. Following on this particular line of comparison, we can see that this, his final publication, continues the concern with the personal, seen in the Burton biography, but in this last instance the spotlight is focused on the author himself.

Occasionally Eric remarked to me that far too many historians tend to hide behind a cloak of anonymity. It is as if they had no other attributes, or, at least, if they had, then these had no bearing whatsoever on their historical judgements, unless such attributes were only of a safe, permitted kind. For example, during the controversy of a generation ago, between Eric Hobsbawm and Max Hartwell in regard to living standards during the Industrial Revolution, Eric was always indignant when Hobsbawm was described as a Marxist historian whilst it was tacitly assumed that Hartwell was politically untainted. How healthy it would be for academic scholarship if all notable historians underwent the equivalent to a session with Dr. Anthony Clare in his radio series, 'In the Psychiatrist's Chair'. Appropriately, this present book puts a formative phase of Eric Sigsworth's life under the microscope.

It is clear that the intention of these reminiscences is to be neither an account of the 1930s in a provincial locality nor a straightforward slice of

Montague Burton: The Tailor of Taste, (Manchester University Press, 1990)

autobiography. It is rather an exploration of the effect that a certain district in south Leeds had on Eric during most of his school years. This district, Beeston, Eric describes as respectable working-class. Certainly it was superior to many parts of its immediate neighbours, Holbeck and Hunslet. This brand of respectability carried with it varying if not opposing values: self-sufficiency, thrift and perseverance; yet narrowness of outlook, disdain for the socially inferior, and excessive respect for those above. For anyone who knew Eric the varied effects of such values, both positive and negative, could be seen in many of his most obvious characteristics: compassion, joviality, generosity, out-goingness, and political radicalism.

As to the text itself, these reminiscences are highly personal yet directed by a qualified intellect. At the same time, formality and rigidity are given a wide berth: things sometimes unfortunately associated with academic rigour. The various parts were hand-written over a number of years; and the final parts were compiled under very adverse physical circumstances in the last months of Eric's life. The original text has passed into the possession of Eric's son, Michael, himself a highly qualified historian. When I mention lack of formality in the text, I imply no lapse from high standards but rather a text devoid of cited references and notes, and hardly a mention of any conventional historical framework; at the same time, this is in no way a run-of-the-mill local history. Eric knew full well all the horrors of antiquarianism. He was far too experienced a hand to fall into the many easy traps which unfortunately still prove so beguiling, especially in this particular genre.

It is clear to readers that Eric made no attempt to write as if he were creating a child's diary, yet at the same time he evokes the world of childhood with its many confusions, evasions and contradictions. What is more, he produces some very illuminating insights into the processes of historical continuity and change. For example, he remarks on the backward-looking traditional diet, and the forward-looking connection between the new, small (often one-child) family and excessive domestic spick-and-spanness. He reveals in a personal and natural way certain points where the nineteenth century persisted into the inter-war period, and, alternatively, where the modern world was already established. However, it is mainly the subtleties, the asides, and the all-pervasive humour that make up my lasting impression of this work. These are the ready devices that Eric uses to expose personal experience, and, in this way, to illustrate historical change as well as some of its sticking-points. The contents of this book provide a useful complement to Eric's output over a long and productive academic lifetime.

I ought to add that my own roots are similar to those of Eric, but with some interesting differences. My working-class inner suburb was to the east of Leeds centre, not south, as in Eric's case. Whereas Eric had to cross the River Aire in order to visit the town centre, I had to skirt Quarry Hill Flats (a tribute to European modernism, now long consigned to the ashes of history). Whilst Eric still sensed the long shadow of the First World War, I, being slightly, but in this case significantly, younger, grew up with the threat and eventual actuality of the Second. Thus, for me, Eric's book conjures up some memories that are closely akin to his, yet also stirs areas of difference, if not of total contrast. Things such as these make reading personal work of this standard so rewarding.

Eric's evocation has a timeless quality. It will stir memories in the ways I have suggested, but for others it will open doors on to a world of not so long ago. It is a tribute to the author that he declares himself so honestly: not common in his profession.

Jim Leonard,
formerly Reader in Local History,
Teeside Polytechnic
(now University of Teeside)

Overhead wires, Briggate

By courtesy of Leeds Leisure Services

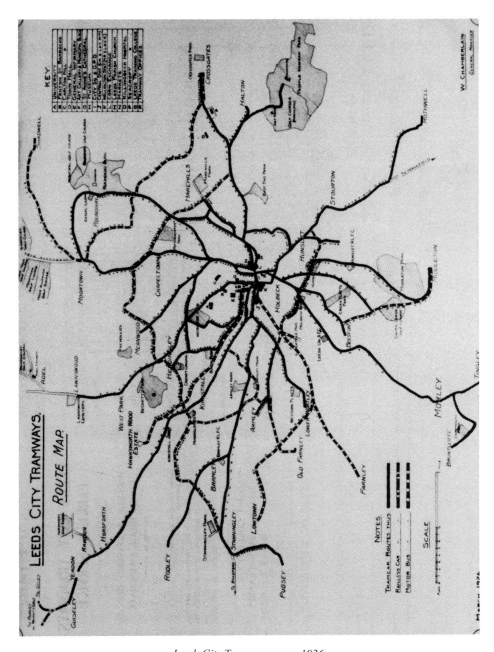

Leeds City Tramways map, 1926

By courtesy of Yorkshire Evening Post

Prologue – The 'Thirties

The 'thirties, as I remember them, were not a bad decade. The economic depression by-passed us. My father, a hairdresser, escaped unemployment, so we were better-off at the end of the decade than we had been when it opened. In another way we personified the textbooks by being part of the building boom. So the memories which are recorded here are not those of a poverty-stricken childhood. Not that we were rich: I do not know what my father earned. There were tips, of course, which boosted his income and served as a constant reminder of his servile status in society. Whatever his wages amounted to they did not reach the bench-mark of the 'five pounds a week man'. This explains why we spent so much time listening to Radio Athlone, to the draw of the Irish Hospitals Sweepstake – first prize, £30,000, or hunched over the table doing the Pools. We never won anything, but on Wednesday nights it seemed possible and we each constructed fantasy worlds of what we would do if . . . In fact, our forecasts bore little relation to reality.

There was little to remind us of the real poverty endured by many in this time of high unemployment. Beeston, the suburb in which we lived, lay between Holbeck and Hunslet, upon a hill. It was there that slums abounded and poverty flourished. But with no pressing need to visit them they remained out of sight and out of mind. Lurid stories about the activities of the de-bugging van always concerned Holbeck or Hunslet, never Beeston. Sometimes we would encounter bands of children in summer, visiting the park. You could tell where they came from by their clothing. I am sorry to say that we behaved very badly towards them. There is no snobbery worse than that of members of the next rung upwards in society to those below them.

Our crass behaviour, I suppose, had its roots in ignorance and fear. These characterised our attitudes to international affairs. Bombs could rain down on Guernica, the Japanese could invade Manchuria, the Italians could admire the explosion of their bombs among Abyssinian tribesmen. We remained unmoved. They had nothing to do with us. When the government gave out gas masks and Mr. Bradley, over the road, began to build an air-raid shelter, not waiting for officialdom to provide an Anderson shelter, we knew 'something was up'. The free issue of gas masks set the seal on things. Far from reassuring many that they were a wise precaution, they confirmed their fears of an imminent extinction. Not the least thing about them was their capacity for converting the most familiar and loved faces into a

1

nightmare parody, in which everybody looked alike. They also made a farting noise, ensuring that it was hard to take anyone seriously.

So the 1930s ended in the 'phoney war'. It had been a decade of falling prices and heavy unemployment. This book is not about them. Nor is it an autobiography. On its hill, flanked by its neighbours Hunslet and Holbeck, Beeston had been developed much later and was recognisably a village. Its growth was delayed until the turn of the eighteenth century. It thus escaped the worst of the effects of early industrialisation which had swept like a plague over the erstwhile fields surrounding Hunslet and Holbeck, covering them with an unregulated or ill-regulated mass of houses, indiscriminately mixed with factories. Beeston developed within the framework of comprehensive bye-laws decreeing what should be built and where. The result was a community of decent, predominantly working-class housing, with only a jam factory and an engineering works intruding. Beeston escaped the worst of the Depression, had no slums to clear and contributed to the housing boom of the 'thirties. Hunslet and Holbeck, with their masses of slums, attracted the most vulnerable members of society, to whom low rents were a magnet, and, in contrast, displayed greater hardship.

Beeston in the 'thirties, if our street was anything to go by, was a smug, narrow-minded society. Solidly working class, it returned a Tory M.P. and city councillor. Its main social centre was the Conservative Club. It prospered quietly. This book explores its impact on a growing boy. It might have been worse . . .

School group, 1930s

By courtesy of Yorkshire Evening Post

2

CHAPTER 1
Tram Routes

The trams which ran through Headingley to Lawnswood always seemed superior to those which served other parts of Leeds. It was on this route that the latest models were introduced, with upholstered seats instead of the slatted wooden kind which gave spine-jarring accommodation on the other routes. Vehicles of this size could hardly have pretensions to be stream-lined, but the designers of the new trams which went to Lawnswood had trimmed them to give this impression. On reaching the terminus the conductor simply pulled a rope to change the direction of the device connecting the tram to the electrified wire overhead. On the older types of tram he did this with a long bamboo pole, causing a display of blue flashes. He then switched round all the seats to face the opposite direction. The driver changed ends and after an interval the tram was ready to return to the city centre.

The Headingley trams also served the suburbs of Harehills, Roundhay and Moortown, speeding along the express track past Gipton Woods and across the wide spaces of Soldiers' Field, carrying passengers to a day out in Roundhay Park. For a small sum it was possible to travel southwards from Lawnswood into the city centre, where City Square was vibrant with the metallic clanging and groanings of trams; where also, in the early evenings, crowds queued to be despatched in all directions to their suburbs. From City Square the same tram ground its way eastwards along Boar Lane, making a spectacular left turn into Briggate, where more queues waited in the middle of the street, between the two streams of traffic, barely sheltered from the weather by a green cast-iron structure, in which, at rush hours, it was easy to join the wrong queue. From Briggate the route went past the exotic-seeming Jewish shops and establishments, like the offices of a Jewish newspaper, and also a small park which was politely known as the Jews' Park, and up the Harrogate Road past the erstwhile village of Chapel Allerton to Moortown, the outermost suburb in that direction. At Moortown corner, the tram made a sharp right turn along Street Lane to Roundhay Park and so across Soldiers' Field, through Gipton and Harehills, the houses becoming smaller as the City centre was approached. Then, one arrived back in City Square and so, back again, out to Lawnswood. There was nothing to prevent an enthusiast transversing the city, back and forth during the entire time that the tram was on duty, sitting upstairs in the front seat amid a mounting pile of tram tickets.

3

There was a story that one wretched student at the University, which the tram passed on its outward journey towards Lawnswood, found himself on the morning of his final examinations in the grip of a mental blockage so compelling that he was incapable of movement as the tram reached the appropriate stop. Gripped by the terror of the unknown ordeal ahead, he remained fixed in his seat, his legs refusing to function as the tram disgorged its noisy load of students blessed with greater confidence than he. And so he travelled on all the way to Lawnswood, where he paid his fare back to the University. Arriving there he was late, by now, for the start of his examination and therefore seized by an even greater sense of panic and even less capable of dismounting. How many times he went round the city, what passed between him and an incredulous conductor, how much he spent on fares – all these and other details have been lost. At the end of the tram's spell of duty, when the driver piloted his vehicle into the depot where it would spend the night, his faithful passenger remained and was only persuaded to leave under expert medical guidance. He was the nearest thing to the Flying Dutchman in the annals of Leeds City Transport Department.

An altogether inferior and older class of rolling stock plied for hire on our route. The Number 5 tram which linked our suburb with central Leeds and beyond had its lower deck reserved for non-smokers and those incapable of climbing the steeply curving metal stairs ascending to the upper deck. A lingering social tradition, perhaps allied to these segregative factors, resulted in the lower deck being mainly patronised by women and girls, though among these were those enslaved by tobacco and possessed with the physical and moral courage to invade the upper deck. Here there were three choices. The upper deck was open at each end. The desire for fresh air could therefore be gratified, either to the fullest extent at the front, pleasant on a warm day in summer, but almost lethal in colder weather. Or, less vigorously, at the rear-end between these breezy extremities, was a sheltered compartment with sliding doors and enclosed in glass. In here the air was usually so smoky that thrifty passengers saved money by not lighting up, merely breathing deeply. A well-lit pipe could fumigate the passengers whose clothes would stink for days. Combined with the lurching of the tram it could soon induce nausea.

One fierce little man who drove a horse and cart, delivering coal for the Co-op, smoked such an aggressive pipe-full of thick twist that no one would sit near him. Isolated in clouds of evil-smelling smoke he sat darting suspicious and angry glances at his fellow passengers who appeared to be ostracising him. It was a period when the manufacturers of Lifebuoy carbolic-scented soap had recently made the public aware of the dangers of 'B.O.', but it was his pipe which was to blame, though it must be said that prolonged contact with horses was a contributory cause of his isolation. Even in his absence, the concentration of smoke made it a noxious journey in a city which was notorious for the high incidence of bronchial diseases.

On a fair day in summer, however, with the breeze created by the moving tram rippling one's shirt, there was no better way to travel than at the front end of the upper deck. Master of the passing scene, one shared the joys of driving, if only in spirit, with the driver, whose unseen but audible and abrasive presence was concealed directly below.

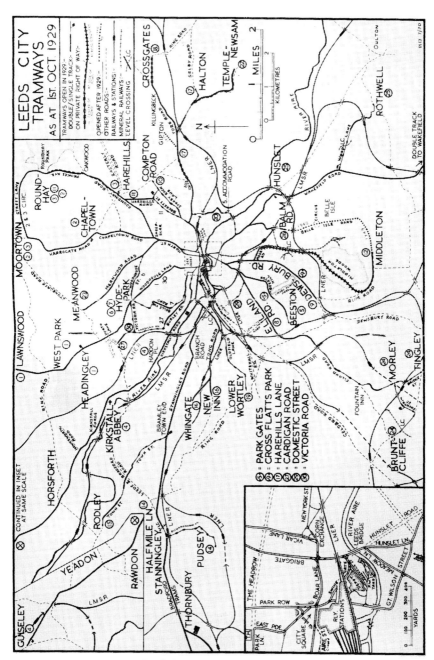

Leeds City Tramways Map, 1929.
By courtesy of Yorkshire Evening Post

The city of Leeds was covered by a network of tramlines, radiating from the central depot in Swinegate. All the main roads out of the city were also the principal tramway arteries. At their junctions the air was congested with a tangle of overhead wires supplying electric power, and discordant with the harsh metallic sound of iron wheels grating on iron rails. Usually the trams mixed as freely with the rest of the traffic as their fixed tracks would allow, the lines being laid in two parallel sets down the middle of the road, creating also a hazard for cyclists. The trams' restricted manoevrability was less of a problem when motor vehicle traffic was less prone to congestion. Sometimes, in more recently developed suburbs there were specially segregated express tracks fenced-off by the side of the road. In general, however, their trundling presence could be accommodated, like that of horse-drawn carts of all sizes and types which still abounded in the streets.

Many firms presumably still found it economical to deliver their goods by horse-drawn vehicles rather than by motor-van. The railway companies sent parcels by a fleet of carts radiating from their stations. Leeds Industrial Co-operative society, or the Co-op as it was popularly known, had an armada of coal carts, the two men in charge of each perched on the front, protected in wet weather by empty coal sacks draped across their shoulders, white eyes and teeth and pink lips unnaturally prominent in their blackened faces. The larger distributors, amongst whom the Co-op was probably the biggest, similarly delivered milk by horse and cart, though there were still small suppliers in the suburbs using smaller floats. In these the milk was carried in large metal cans from which it was ladled into the customers' jugs. The ladles were pint-sized or measured out a gill [¼ pint] of milk.

Greengrocers commonly toured the streets, their wares piled up attractively on flat carts with green canvas awnings. As in the shops, the finer specimens of fruit were at the front of the pile, artfully concealing older scruffier goods at the rear, from which the unwary customer was served. These were only the main, regular visitors to the streets. In addition, there was a variety of other small traders – hawkers, rag-and-bone men, sellers of firewood and others – with all kinds of vehicles, drawn by creatures ranging from lively ponies known as 'galloways' or 'gallowers', to sad old horses suffering from deeply curved spines, unable to do more than amble dispiritedly down the road. The only time they became more animated was when, over a garden wall, they caught sight of something green and edible. Then, if the driver was engaged with a customer, they would gently edge towards the object of their desire. The most distinguished turnouts, however, were owned by the breweries. Laden with barrels and crates, drawn by matched pairs of magnificent Shire horses, they delivered beer to public houses, off-licensed shops and private customers. Their crews, who managed the heavy and dangerous-looking work of loading the full barrels into the pub cellars with ropes and pulleys, became increasingly mellow as each landlord treated them to a sample of the product. Special mention must be made of the spanking delivery vans operated by Ringtons, the tea retailers: box-like contraptions decorated in black, green and gold and drawn by a single horse, spirited enough to move at a brisk trot. Their main depot was not far away, so they were a familiar sight.

The sweet smell of horse-sweat, the rich aroma of their droppings, the prolific cascades of steaming horse-piss, the sound of their hooves, jingle of harness and rumbling of iron-shod wheels, were all part of their contribution to the life of the streets. Visible evidence of their passing in the form of piles of golden-brown balls was highly prized by the owners of the small gardens along their route. Lurking expectantly behind twitching lace curtains, they would rush out, bucket and set-pot shovel in hand, to capture the still steaming pile [a set-pot was a coal fired boiler to heat water for washing clothes, described in Chapter 2]. It was reputed to be very good for rhubarb – a popular, if melancholy-looking crop. Speed was essential, or the prize would be taken away by small boys, already afflicted by the stirrings of the capitalistic spirit, to be sold for one penny per bucketful. Doubtless, they little realised that their activities were directly descended from those of Henry Mayhew's 'pure finders' [collectors of dog faeces] in the London streets of the mid-nineteenth century. Actual 'pure finders' were not in evidence in the Leeds streets in the 1930s, though an uncle recalled them in Armley searching the streets and the piece of ground known optimistically as the Gaol Field, where there were plentiful supplies of dog turds. However, this was a memory of the years before the First World War. The product was sold by the bucketful to tanneries, of which there were plenty in Leeds, and used in them to soften the leather.

The only other cash crop which the streets yielded was cigarette stubs, especially at strategic points, like tram stops and outside public houses and the surroundings of football grounds, as at Elland Road or Parkside, the local homes respectively of Leeds United and Hunslet Rugby League Football Club. It was possible, of course, to buy very cheap cigarettes in thin paper packets of five, with Woodbines being the most popular, followed by Weights, Robins and Black Cat. Obliging tobacconists would even sell them singly to the really poor, but below even this level of consumption was the free bounty of the streets – the 'dog end'. These were mainly collected by old men, shuffling along with downcast eyes scanning the pavement. Put in a tin box, they were dismembered, and the tobacco which remained rolled in cigarette papers, making thin knobbly-looking cigarettes which were smoked sparingly – to avoid leaving any butt ends. A pin was used to extract the utmost smoke.

Anyone wishing to travel beyond Leeds cheaply and with little effort could penetrate by tram into the West Riding and beyond. Travelling westwards from the city, climbing through Armley and Bramley, the terminus of the Leeds system was below the railway viaduct in Stanningley. Here, as at some frontier post, one made a simple change to the waiting Bradford tram just along the road, its crew wearing alien peaked caps made of mottled woven straw. And so, with a sense of adventure mounting with each stage of the descent into Bradford, one changed trams again to make the ascent to Queensbury's chilly heights. Another change to yet another company's transport brought one to the middle of Halifax, and another change of trams to the Calder valley and towards the Lancashire border.

Or there were foreign trams which enjoyed the privilege of using the Leeds lines into the city centre. Ancient-looking, their battered green paint conspicuous against the dark blue and cream of the Leeds trams, they came groaning and limping from the south, linking Leeds and Wakefield. With the exercise of a little ingenuity much of the West Riding and the towns of industrial Lancashire were within reach, provided one could tolerate this slow and stately form of transport.

The age of trams was in fact a brief episode in urban development in this country, yet, looking back, these lumbering giants seemed to be a permanent feature of towns. In some towns they had gothic roofs to accommodate their passage through the arches of ancient town walls. Yet they survived only a few years beyond the end of the Second World War. In Leeds, the last tram, suitably decorated with electric light bulbs, clanked into oblivion in the late 1950s. It was not a failure to respond to the demands of modernisation which brought about their end – new models were constantly being introduced and tramway systems still flourish on the Continent. A step towards cost-saving was the introduction of a new ticket machine. Previously the conductor carried a rack of tickets of different colours – pale green for a halfpenny fare, blue for a penny, and so on. The tickets were serially numbered and to receive one with numbers adding up to twenty-one was a portent of great good fortune. Some collected tram tickets with the avidity devoted by others to postage stamps, or tin soldiers, matchboxes, or whatever inflamed their acquisitive appetites. It seemed a dull form of endeavour, like collecting car numbers or train spotting. Perhaps it brought keener satisfaction when embracing the tickets of other towns, or even foreign tickets. The new ticket machines, self-inking devices, were ingenious, but a disappointment for the collector. Gone were the variously coloured thin cardboard strips with advertisements on the back. Instead, a setting of dials, a winding of the handle and a whirring sound replaced the cheerful ring of the hand punch. The result was a feebly printed piece of paper, fed from an inner magazine. Hardly the sort of thing for the collector to enthuse about. Whether new or old the tickets were a constant source of anxiety. The appearance of an Inspector set off a nervous scramble through one's pockets which, as likely as not, would only produce tickets of former journeys. There followed a frantic scrabbling amongst the discarded tickets on the floor. This was especially humiliating where there were two rows of seats facing one another, as they did on the older trams, and one pursued one's search under the scrutiny of one's fellow passengers.

Whatever might thus be the perils to dignity were offset by the safety and reliability of the tram. Forever fixed in their tracks they could not skid and advanced inexorably through the thickest of fog, which, before smoke control legislation, could be dense and smokey. The driver heralded his approach by stamping on a warning bell. The worst thing to happen was when, in very cold weather, the points froze at important junctions. There was an accumulation of trams like so many stranded whales until some official unfroze the points with a can of hot water.

There is, of course, a Tramways Museum at Crich in Derbyshire, where nostalgia can be indulged and the finer points of comparison made between the different types of tram, painted in the various civic colours of the towns which they served. As a spectacle it could never equal that of tens of hundreds of trams (or so it seemed) abandoned and waiting silently along the whole length of Low Fields Road and round the bend into Elland Road, as the gloom of a late winter afternoon deepened and, behind the high walls and embankments of Leeds United football ground, the crowd alternately roared in exultation and groaned in agony. The cold wind sang in the overhead wires. The litter of waste paper fluttered and swirled. Solidly built, like metallic prehistoric monsters, the trams awaiting the crowds of spectators suggested permanence. There was nothing to indicate that they would soon be scrapped for ever.

The daily journey to school by tram started at the top of the street, on what was known locally as The Common. The name was perhaps a vestige of a distant past before a stretch of common land was engulfed by the expansion of the city. Now it was simply a main road with a patch of dog-infested grass along part of its length, a parade of shops and, at right angles to it, row after row of back-to-back houses. The Parkfields, the Cross Flats, the Marleys and Nosters, among others, the collective names concealing Street, Road, Row, Grove, Place, Avenue and so on, as variants around a basic theme. Whoever was responsible for naming streets – that genius who had a sufficient sense of irony to name Prosperity Street, or the Danubes in Holbeck, or the Fertiles and Nippets in Burmantofts, usually thought up some prefix to which these permutations could be tagged on. It was a faltering in municipal ingenuity which was presumably responsible for naming streets in Wortley, First Avenue and so on, up to Eighteenth Avenue where the Railway Mission was to be found, with my grandparents as resident caretakers. Or was it in emulation of the practice followed in New York?

The next stop on the way into town was outside the back entrance to Holbeck Cemetery on one side of the road; a collection of *Memento Mori* ranging from aldermanic pomp down to the plain rows of tombstones marking the last resting place of the paupers who died in the Workhouse. On the other side of the road were the main gates of Cross Flatts Park, intended to shut people out after dusk and supplemented by high spiked railings. There would be no goings-on in that park after dark. In the evenings a curfew bell warned late strollers that the park was about to close and uniformed park rangers ensured that its message was observed.

For those still allowed to be out after the park had closed, the streets remained as a playground offering varied possibilities. To begin with, there were the gas lamps, still being lit, before they were controlled by an automatic switch, by a lamplighter who walked the streets carrying a long pole. This, when applied inside the lamp, lit the mantle, throwing a pool of yellow light into the gathering darkness. It was, of course, possible to anticipate this by giving the base of the standard a good kick, but the lamplighter regarded this as a usurpation of his function.

The horizontal bar to prop ladders against could also be used to fix a rope to, for a swing. This too was unpopular with the authorities. Too many bodies clinging to the rope bent the bar. Above all, it was the lamp itself which was, the attraction. Its light brought children out of the night like moths. Several versions of 'hide and seek' revolved around it. First there would be a 'dip' – each player standing in a circle, both fists extended. In the middle, the child doing the 'dip' began a chant, touching each fist in time to the rhythm:

"One potato, two potato, three potato, four,
Five potato, six potato, seven potato more"
or:

9

"As I was going down Icky Picky Lane
    I met some Icky Picky Peee--pul..."
or more daringly:
    "Nebuchadnezzar, king of the Jews,
    Wiped his bum on the *Evening News* . . ."
and:
    "Eeny, meeny, miny, mo,
    Sit the baby on the po.
    When it's done,
    Wipe its bum.
    Eeny, meeny, miny mo."
Whatever might be the jingle, however naughty the words, it invariably
ended with:
    "And if you do not want to play
    Take hook and go away
    With a raggle taggle dishcloth
    Out goes YOU."
The owner of the fist struck on the word "YOU" was 'it' or 'on' and would
have to seek out the others from their hiding places. The child who was 'on'
stood facing the lamp-post and counted to one hundred and one. As he
reached this figure, he would shout a warning:
    "Coming to seek all over
    Hiddy or not!"
And so the hunt began. A variant of simple 'Hide-and-Seek' was called
'Relieve-O'. Those who had been caught waited in the circle of lamplight
and could be released if one of the remainder, yet to be detected, got back
to the lamp post shouting Relieve-O, which freed the captives to hide again.
It was a game which could go on all night.

Before darkness fell the street was the scene of different ball games,
according to the season. In the football season the most popular pitches were
up against the wall of the end house in a row, on which were chalked
goalposts, while last season's wickets were allowed to fade. These were
unpopular activities with the inhabitants of the end houses. There were
windows to be broken and the tiny gardens had owners who voiced strong
objections to the arrival in them of either a football or a cricket ball – not that
our cricket balls were the polished red leather version of proper matches. The
nearest we got was an imitation cork ball, painted red. Otherwise we made
do with old tennis balls, or any ball was pressed into service. Beginning with
threats: "I'll tell yer father!", or "I'll fetch t'bobby!", punitive action could
result in the confiscation of the ball by the offended householder. Those who
lived in end houses failed to realise that the dull thuds against their wall
deserved tumultuous applause rather than niggling criticism.

Such encounters could easily degenerate. The more belligerent the
householder the greater the danger of this. The satisfaction derived from acts
of hostility increased in proportion to the fury they evoked, culminating in
the triumph of being chased. A really successful campaign could even
involve parents. Whatever might be the painful end-product in the privacy
of one's own home, following a complaint of unruly behaviour, parents were
often quick to defend their offspring against slanderous attacks in the public
theatre of the street.

CHAPTER 2

Housing

Once the tram had left the park and cemetery there followed a sharp descent down the steeply curving track of Beeston Hill. At the top, as the tram paused to pick up passengers there was a brief panoramic view of the whole city and beyond. On a clear day one could see across the Aire valley with its industrial crowding to open country. The tram plunged downhill past the Malvern cinema with its neon sign centred on a clock tower. Beneath the clock an illuminated neon pendulum flashed to and fro – an innovation of the 1930s. On the right, in the same row, a large new building provided accommodation for itinerant workers passing through the city. Built and administered by the local authority it gave a superior form of shelter to that otherwise available in cheap lodging houses and doss houses. It was intended as a haven for those travelling the country in search of work.

At the bottom of the hill and on the other side of the road stood the grim institution housing those for whom the chronic poverty of old age, or some other catastrophe, meant resorting to the Workhouse. It was divided into two halves by a high railing which segregated the two sexes. The men wore cloth caps and grey, ill-fitting suits of shoddy material. The women wore white aprons over their dresses. On fine days they stood about or sat on forms opposite their dormitories, a chilling and uncomfortable sight. They were paupers, failures in life, outcasts. At night the windows of their dormitories, curtained only on the lower half, showed a low wattage, unshaded light bulb burning in each ward. The sight must have provoked dispiriting reflections in the minds of many passengers passing quickly by in the tram, given the widespread insecurity of the times and the poverty which dominated the immediately surrounding area. The paupers were buried in Holbeck Cemetery on the top of the hill, in common graves, in rows set apart from the rest, easily distinguished by the number of unrelated names recorded on the same headstone.

This was one of the oldest working-class parts of Leeds, the houses becoming more crowded and decrepit the further down the hill one travelled towards the city centre. Not that there was really much to be seen from the tram of the squalor and poverty of its mean streets. The main road was lined by a facade of shops and the streets were thus concealed. To be sure, the shops were poor enough, catering as they did for that district, but their variety and, for some, their eye-catching displays, made them appear less poverty-stricken than the streets stretching acre by acre behind them – streets never intended for occupation by anyone other than the poor. Large parts of Leeds were being demolished and much of this area was condemned, only to be reprieved by the outbreak of war and consequent restrictions on house building which followed during the 1940s and early 1950s. During this period of a decade and a half, knowing their properties were going to be demolished, landlords were reluctant to spend money on repairs. Already wretched abodes in the 1930s, they therefore underwent further deterioration unchecked.

At one particular point the tram passed a space unshielded by shops, providing a full view of working-class housing built early in the nineteenth century. A square asphalted space surrounded by iron railings had been provided as a playground by some charity. Bounded by the main road one side, it was surrounded on the other three by dismal rows of slum houses. A scene of vigorous activity on fine days and evenings, it was called Mutton Hill and celebrated in a local ditty:

"Burglar Bill of Mutton Hill
Never worked and never will.
When he worked, it was a wonder
'Cos he only worked on Sunday."

Just before the tram reached Mutton Hill it passed, on the same side, the domed building of the Queen's cinema and music hall, which had a stage and presented live entertainment on occasion (Ivor E. Keys), though this had been superseded by the insubstantial pageant of the silver screen. And so, past the hovels on Sweet Street to the junction of Meadow Lane with Victoria Road. Here, depending on its eventual destination, the tram either turned left, heading for City Square, past the mills and factories of the oldest part of industrial Leeds by the side of the Holbeck (which had provided water power), over Victoria Bridge, underneath the City Station, through the Dark Arches. Alternatively, it proceeded along Meadow Lane to Leeds Bridge and Lower Briggate, following the traditional route into town. As its name implies, it had once been a lane which passed between meadows, connecting the villages of Beeston and Holbeck with Leeds and bringing traffic from the thriving woollen-producing area to the Cloth Hall which provided trestles on which the domestic clothier could display his hand-woven pieces of cloth for the scrutiny of the merchants of Leeds. There were still, along it, a few mouldering cottages and yards which recalled a bucolic past, but otherwise it was a grimly industrial thoroughfare dominated by a huge foul-smelling gas works.

A point of interest was one of the churches built by the Church of England in the aftermath of the Napoleonic Wars with the aid of a Parliamentary grant, intended to stem the Godlessness of the urban working classes. If Horace Mann's religious census of 1851 is to be believed, it had enjoyed indifferent success and Christ Church was now increasingly redundant as much of the population it was designed to cater for was being dispersed to distant suburban locations as a result of the slum clearance schemes. The church, soot-blackened neo-Gothic, was an increasingly sad object. Further in towards the city was another reminder of its social history, a tablet commemorating the victims of the 1831 cholera epidemic, subsequently

12

By courtesy of Leeds Leisure Services

"Let Burton Dress You!", Briggate, Leeds.

moved, I believe, to a location on Hunslet Moor.

Near the end of the journey another plaque on the side of one of the buildings on Leeds Bridge was to rescue from oblivion the Rev. Jabez Tunnicliffe who had created the Band of Hope. This temperance organisation was aimed particularly at children, in the belief that indoctrination when young would result in a lifetime's sobriety, so that they could forever sing one of the Band's favourite hymns:

"My drink is water bright,
Water bright, water bright
From the crystal spring."

Actually, in the sanitary circumstances in the middle years of the nineteenth century, when the Band of Hope was founded, they would have been ill-advised to drink water, with the risk of catching some horrible disease like cholera.

From the bridge itself there was a fine view of the warehouses and wharves built to cater for the traffic at the western end of the Aire and Calder Navigation, the city's main economic artery in the pre-railway age. On the immediate approaches to the bridge were several shops. One was very glamorous in the eyes of small boys, being a sports outfitters belonging to the legendary Yorkshire and England cricketer, Herbert Sutcliffe. Another responded to the prevailing economic depression by selling assorted junk, proclaiming, "We Don't Cut Prices – We Murder 'Em". A third was a firm of herbalists offering natural cures for all manner of diseases. "Stop That Itching" commanded a sign over the shop. A carton of their famous ointment would do the trick. Above the shop next door was a sign which – having been conditioned by the peremptory tone of the herbalist's command – one read as an equally compelling instruction. It read "Die Stamping". It could, when pondered over, produce mental images confused enough to interfere with normal mundane concerns. Such a defiant end to life! Other shop signs were expressed with similar ambiguity. Butchers proclaimed that they were "Family Butchers". Others, of a more radical persuasion, claimed to be "High Class Family Butchers". There was a mystifying sign outside a removal firm reading, "Let Us Quote You" and "Distance No Object".

After the bridge it was a short run up Lower Briggate to alight at the Fifty Shilling Tailors, next door to a building with a strange dream-like quality about it. This was Dyson's jewellery shop which, on top of a turret, had a Time Ball which moved vertically on a projecting metal bar. The movement of the ball was regulated according to Greenwich Mean Time. The name of the tailor's branch shop reflected the rough rule-of-thumb in the trade, that the price of a man's suit should be roughly equal to a working man's weekly wage. On the opposite corner a branch of an even bigger chain of men's tailors carried in its windows a picture of its chairman and founder with the ambiguous message, "Let Burton Dress You".

Street life could be equally dramatic. 'Mischief night' – the fourth of November , was, of course, the classic occasion for settling scores, real or imagined. It had an added zest, given an armoury of fireworks which had been on sale for weeks in anticipation of the Fifth of November. For one halfpenny would buy a 'Little Demon' which, exploded under an empty can, would lift it to an impressive height. Dropped in a letter box it was guaranteed to shock the inhabitants. It was also very effective where the road was as yet unpaved. Many still were, in Beeston, where signs of the 1930s housing boom were widely evident, with the building of new houses outrunning the local authority's capacity for paving the streets which they created. Early November saw such roads thick with mud. A 'Little Demon', not to mention a 'Thunderflash' costing one penny, placed upright opposite the windows of an unpopular householder, would splatter them with mud. This was particularly offensive in an area where the matrons were aggressively house-proud, spending large amounts of their time in swilling garden paths, washing windows and scouring steps and window sills with 'Donkey Brown' scouring stone.

Actually, in Beeston in the 1930s, the easier practice was creeping in of painting external stonework. It was a labour-saving device, regarded, as were all such, as a symptom of moral degeneracy by the older generation of housewives who continued to patronise the man who came weekly with a contraption pulled by a pony and selling 'Donkey Brown' stone, 'Dolly Blues', 'Dolly Creams' and a variety of harsh chemical preparations for wash day. He was known as 'The Acdo Man'. Dolly Creams were used to give a good colour to the lace net curtains which adorned most windows. Most of the other products were intended to produce that most desired housewifely attainment, a lineful of washing so dazzling in its whiteness that it drew admiring comment. Hanging out the washing in a densely populated district, with each house having a coal fire, was a perilous business, especially on a windless day, when the smoke spilled straight down. On such a day the washing was ruined by being peppered with a myriad sooty specks. It was best on such days to vanish discreetly until the effects of such a catastrophe had been dissipated.

In fact wash-days were best avoided. In such small houses, in the absence of washing machines, the work was done in a big zinc tub with a device known as a 'posser' [a bell-shaped piece of metal with holes in, on a wooden handle, used to agitate the wet clothes] and the clean washing wrung out through a mangle – a great cast-iron frame carrying a pair of heavy wooden rollers turned by heavy geared wheels and a handle. It was hard work, producing short maternal tempers, and in any case the steam which had a bad habit of condensing on the walls, and the smell of wet washing permeating the whole house made life miserable.

In the poorest areas of the city there were municipal wash houses to which the wash could be taken, usually in an empty pram, but they were not patronised from our street. Firstly, they were tainted with an aura of poverty. Secondly, they were too far away. At the other extreme it was too expensive to have the laundry collected by a commercial firm. So Monday continued to be dominated by the sound of 'possing' and the rumble of the mangle. This domination could last through Tuesday in winter or wet weather when the clothes could not be hung out to dry. Instead they were hung on a clothes horse and dried round the living-room fire. Not only did their presence take up precious space in those small rooms, but, by the very nature of the act, the drying clothes effectively blocked off the heat of the fire. So one sat, cramped and cold, contemplating the steam rising from the washing. And this was not all. After washing came starching and ironing and then once again the clothes were draped over the horse by the fire for airing. To add to the labour, most households did not possess an electric iron, but used instead heavy flat-irons which had to be heated in the oven or on a gas ring and held with a protective cloth on the hand. Starching before ironing added yet another stage to the tedium of the operation. The only redeeming thing was that a clothes-horse, up-ended and draped with an old blanket, made a very good tent.

If labour-saving devices had made only slight inroads into the work of the weekly wash, then equally there were not many houses which boasted possession of a vacuum cleaner, which was a prized object. The best and most prestigious were the Hoover cleaners but there were on offer other smaller brands like the Goblin, which made a high whining sound. There were, of course, carpet sweepers which seemed to do little more than push the crumbs around the floor and which, at intervals, disobligingly kicked out their accumulations in a frowzy pile. Otherwise there were dustpans and stiff hand-brushes for carpets and rugs and softer ones for polished surfaces like linoleum and stained floor boards. The problem here was that the greater the energy applied to sweeping the greater was the cloud of dust raised. This was, however, often mitigated by strewing the floor with damp tea leaves before sweeping – in local terms, "sleckin' t'dust". It was doubtless the absence of effective cleaning devices which made it necessary to Spring Clean through the house as they said, "from top to bottom" – an orgy of dusting, scrubbing, washing and polishing which involved moving all the furniture and emptying all the drawers, making the weekly cleansing look very inferior.

All this work, much of it self-defeating, all of it laborious and tedious, was an expression of virtue. Not noted for their Godliness, Beeston matrons sought Grace through being so house-proud that they appeared, in fact, mad. They created homes in which it was impossible to relax, lest an antimacassar should be creased or a fugitive crumb fall on the carpet. There was one house where, even in the most inclement weather, the husband was turned out into the garden at night to smoke his pipe in case he created a mess in the house. As any passer-by could testify, he also took the opportunity to relieve himself of excess wind, standing there in the dark, puffing his pipe and rending the night air with farts. In other houses friends were not allowed inside for fear that they would make the place untidy. Our next door neighbour used a tape measure to place exactly the ornaments and knick-knacks on the mantelpiece. Any new piece of furniture, like an upholstered settee or an armchair, was kept covered in sheets so that it was difficult to know why it had been purchased at all. The greatest praise which could gladden the ear of such a housewife was not that her house was warm and comfortable, friendly or welcoming, but that she kept it "like a little palace", or "band box" and that "you could eat your dinner off the floor". It was a telling indication of the narrowness, the spiritual poverty, the emptiness of the rest of their lives that such women could have become so enslaved by housework. But then, this was the period of having only one child, or none. Most of these women and their husbands had left school at thirteen, like my mother. There is no wonder that housework held such a dominating place in their lives which might otherwise have appeared so barren.

Another change in the external appearance of the house was the colour of the paintwork. Traditionally, doors and window frames were 'grained'. The painter, working basically in dark brown, intending to reproduce oak or walnut colour, displayed his true skill by simulating with brushes and combs, a grain in the wood. His art was then sealed and protected by coats of varnish. Here and there, however, restless spirits sought change. Dark red woodwork began to appear. This was not too great a break with tradition, since it too could be grained to simulate mahogany. But, with even greater daring, a few houses began to be painted in green, even though this risked the censure of stern traditionalists, expressed in comments such as "it looks like a dilly oil". For the expert grainer whose skills had been much in demand, the writing was on the woodwork, if not on the wall, though he was as yet a long way from resorting to the full range of colours in which houses now appear.

Such departures from custom and, indeed, the acquisition of a tool like the vacuum cleaner, and of new furniture, were probably because the houses in which we lived were newly built. Moving from one house to another, especially to a new house, brings a desire for new, more 'modern' things to go in it. Years ago our streets had been laid out but uncompleted as earlier building booms collapsed, leaving unfinished rows of mainly back-to-back houses. These reflected in design and amenities and the width of the streets which they faced the municipal building regulations then in force. Thus, the top half of our street and, parallel to it for several streets on either side, consisted of rows of back-to-back houses. Each house had its W.C situated below ground, reached either from the adjacent cellar door, or from the house door, down two flights of stone steps into the 'area' as it was called.

The houses each had a tiny garden and the house door opened straight into the living room, the focal point of which was a large iron Yorkist range. It had a raised fire grate. On the left hand side of this was a large tank, filled and emptied by hand, in which water was heated, there being no supply of piped hot water. On the right hand side was a large oven, its heat supply controlled by flues and dampers. Most of the metal work was black, kept shining dully by weekly applications of blacklead, but the edges of the metal, the knob of the oven door and various embellishments were bright work requiring a weekly polish with wire wool. The fender enclosing the hearth was a similarly heavy affair of cast iron, but decorated by brass railings and knobs, as was the shield which covered the hole for ashes below the grate. The whole ensemble was completed by various fire-irons – a large poker and tongs, a brush and small shovel on a stand. They all had decorated brass handles and there was usually a copper kettle and a hearth plate which was made of enamel and carried a geometric design or a naturalistic picture of, say, windmills and tulips. All the brass work required cleaning at least once a week. Above the fireplace was a sort of domestic shrine, the mantelpiece, with a dark-coloured plush valance and prized items on it, such as framed photographs and ornaments. In front of the fender was the hearth rug, traditionally made of 'list' – that is, thousands of small tailor's clippings sewed to a canvas backing in patterned arrangements. There were shops which sold such rugs but some women made them from 'fents' – damaged lengths of cloth and cuttings, cut up into the small pieces which were required. It was a very laborious business, cutting and then sewing the pieces through the canvas with twine, and, as such, reached a peak of housewifely virtue.

In some of these houses there was, by the side of the fireplace, a tall cupboard with doors concealing shelves and a sink with a cold water tap which was the sole source of supply. In others, the sink was in the scullery in which, therefore, washing took place – of persons as well as clothes – and such cooking as was not done in the oven or on the fire in the living room. Those houses with cellars had a 'set-pot' heated by a fire to provide hot water for the washing of clothes. In some houses a bath was installed in the scullery in response to the slum clearance schemes of the 1930s. This had been done in my grandma's house by a landlord who was concerned less with improving the quality of his tenants' lives than with forestalling the compulsory acquisition and demolition of his property. The rent was increased, of course, for the privilege of having this amenity. Usually the bath was topped by a wooden lid covered with oilcloth to make a working surface.

The upper floor in such houses was accessible by a steep staircase which curved on itself in the middle. Upstairs comprised the main bedroom which took a double bed and a wardrobe, and a single bedroom with just enough room for a dressing table, in addition to the single bed. Off the tiny landing another door led up a similar flight of stairs to an attic with a ceiling which sloped in conformity with the roof of the house, from the middle to a point, leaving a wall of about two feet high. At its maximum, therefore, it was less than the area covered by the house. Having no form of heating it was bitter cold in winter, and, having only a skylight, it was stifling in summer. The occupation of these rooms depended on the size and sex composition of the family. A small family having, say, up to three children presented no problem, but more than this began to be difficult. If the children were numerous, as was the case in many working-class households, there certainly was a problem. My maternal grandparents had one daughter and seven sons. Propriety demanded that all the boys slept in the attic, including Robert who had a bladder complaint, which meant that he was incontinent. My other grandparents, with five boys and three girls, were not faced with quite so great a tax on their ingenuity, though, God knows, life was not easy. All these problems and difficulties arose from the sheer pressure of numbers on a wholly inadequate size of house, not from problems of poverty, my maternal grandfather being a labourer and the paternal one a railway guard at the peak of his career – until he suffered demotion for joining a strike before the Great War. Small wonder that all my aunts and uncles who married restricted the size of their families.

Being back-to-back houses, any individual house, except those on the end of the row, was surrounded on three sides by three houses. With walls which were far from sound-proof, voices raised in anger, laughter or song, penetrated easily between them. The playing of a piano, or a wireless or radiogram with the volume turned up above the level of a whisper was equally audible. The only hope of not being assailed from different sides by competing programmes was if everyone was listening to the same offering. Home carpentry or things like shoe repairing were equally intrusive, adding intolerable dimensions of unwanted noise.

By courtesy of Leeds Leisure Services

Tramlines and back-to-back houses.

Such properties, probably built any time during the nineteenth century, or in the early years of the present century, were, in the language of the estate agent, particularly if built since about 1880, "good class scullery houses". They were certainly superior to those built earlier in the evolution of local authority bye-laws regulating house building. The earlier the houses had been built the less generous was the provision of water-closets per house. In descending order of generosity, there were houses sharing with next door, houses built in blocks of eight with lavatories provided in a yard between the blocks, usually in the ratio of two per house, and those which had a row of closets at the end of a street of indeterminate length, where the ratio was variable. There were still houses with dry midden privies [without flushing water] in the 1930s, and others with trough water closets, in spite of the inroads made into this squalid legacy by the house clearance programmes of that decade.

Sharing the elementary common decencies of sanitation called for a high degree of tact and forbearance. The door to the yard containing the W.C.s was usually kept locked, not least against rude little boys and dirty old men or perverts of any age. The 'closet key', as it was known, was usually carried on a loop of string, with a used cotton reel threaded on it for greater ease of finding it, and kept on a hook, perhaps behind the house door. A W.C. was allocated to particular houses which were responsible for its cleanliness, taking turns at the scrubbing. The lavatory paper was frequently sheets of newspaper, cut to a manageable size and threaded on a piece of string. Not for the common man or woman the genteel sensation of wiping their bums on proper toilet paper, though this could possess abrasive qualities varying with the degree of shininess and hardness which it had. Izal was particularly strong on these qualities and carried a hectoring message – "Wash your hands" – printed on each perforated leaf. Medicated, it was doubtless superior to newspaper, which, however, was said to have antiseptic qualities in its printer's ink and provided something to read. Izal was, anyway, too expensive for daily use. These shortcomings help to explain why constipation was so common [and the many remedies for this affliction are recalled in Chapter 10]. A visit to the toilet was not something to be lightly undertaken. Think of the hardship in cold weather, or the agonies of a shy person in performing, so obviously, a function which was supposed to be private!

In common with a few other rows of back-to-back houses built in Leeds in the 1930s, our house was an anachronism. The Housing of The Working Classes Act, passed by Parliament in 1909, had forbidden the further building of houses of this design, but some legal loophole in its drafting had allowed them to be built as late as 1936. This, ironically, was exactly when the city was tearing down great areas where the back-to-back house was seen as the worst manifestation of jerry-building and housing deprivation. As the final form of the type, these new back-to-backs were a snook cocked at history. In addition to the two bedrooms and optional attic upstairs there was, off the same landing, a combined bathroom and W.C., with white tiling as an optional extra. Further, the installation of a gas cooker in the kitchen meant that cooking was removed from the living room. Instead of a Yorkist range one could have a smaller fireplace with a tiled surround and hearth, set in a polished wooden frame of the kind more usually found in the sitting room of larger houses. A back-boiler to this fireplace ensured a piped supply of hot water. An additional feature of the house was a window, set in the top half of the door, which had a matching fanlight, and the tops of the windows were decorated in patterned coloured glass in the fashion of the time – pure 'art deco'. There was no damp, dismal 'area' outside, but a small garden, the size of which was determined by the street widths laid down earlier in the century.

Opposite, when we first moved in (the house smelling of a mixture of recently applied plaster, new timber and fresh paint), was an empty building plot, a shallow depression in which people dumped rubbish. It was a very satisfactory place to play in, covered by long grasses in summer and rich in opportunities for building dens, forts and gun emplacements, or digging trenches and dugouts for war games, still re-enacting the First World War. Beyond this hollow was the park. All-in-all therefore, the view from the house was open and pleasant. It became less so when the same speculative builder who had built our houses erected on the 'Hollow' another row, of rather superior 'through' houses. The days of the 'Hollow' as our playground ended bit by bit, as the row of new houses advanced, but, before their completion, what a wonderful place they provided, in their half-completed state. What venues for heady versions of 'Hide-and-Seek' or 'Relieve-O'! Especially when the houses reached that brief stage in their construction when, still lacking doors and fireplaces, the timber joists downstairs were covered with floorboards. Accessible down through the holes in which the fireplaces would fit was a dark, subterranean world through which we could crawl by flashlight, passing under one house after another, via small communicating spaces which had been left for some inscrutable reason. What bliss, hiding fearfully down there, while, above, the builder cursed and swore, knowing that there were trespassers for the prosecuting, but unable to catch them, as they wormed their way to safety, emerging several houses distant.

The builder who had a thick black moustache and wore a stiff collar and a bowler hat – a billycock hat as they were known – lived in a detached house, referred to as a villa, by the side of a lower entrance to the park. He was a weighty man, not physically, but he was a true representative of the forces of petty capitalism and doing well out of his speculation. A staunch member of the local Conservative Club and no less than the local ward Councillor. It is extraordinary that our M.P., also Conservative, should with him, represent a constituency so solidly working class.

CHAPTER 3

The Centre

Having arrived by tram in Leeds' main street, many choices faced the consumer. To begin with, there were the shops themselves, since the city had the reputation of being the main retailing centre of an area stretching across to the coast, south and west into the industrial West Riding and north-east across the border into Durham. Privately owned coaches, bearing the names of operators from places in the North East like Bishop Auckland, Washington, Spennymoor and Darlington brought, on Saturdays, loads of bargain hunters with strange Geordie accents. Arriving in the morning, they spent the day trudging round the shops increasingly laden with the results of their shopping. They had a fish and chip tea at Youngman's emporium – not out of a newspaper, but eaten with a knife and fork at a table with a cloth on it and waitress service, and a pot of tea and bread and butter, and tomato sauce or H.P. Then, pleasantly full, a visit to a cinema or a show at the Empire or the Varieties, or a round of the pubs before setting off for home late at night.

The main shops were on Briggate. There was Woolworth's, still fulfilling its advertised promise to the customer as the 'threepenny and sixpenny store'. There was some cheating, in that a toy camera, for example, was sold at 6d [sixpence] per part, so that the whole thing cost a few shillings. Otherwise, the range of goods sold for 3d or 6d was remarkable. Much favoured was the salted peanut machine, an illuminated and heated drum out of which at intervals came the delicious product, retailed in bags stained with nut oil. Or for 6d there were wire-framed spectacles, which were important to poor people before the age of the National Health Service. Old men and women, my grandfather among them, would stand peering and blinking through lenses of varying strength until they found a pair which brought their blurred world into better focus, with what harm to their eyesight is unknown. The whole store, with its wooden floors, had that unique smell which would enable a blind person to identify Woolworth's in any town in the country. The same was true of Burton's shops. Presumably the explanation was to be found in the use of the same cleaning materials.

Higher up Briggate, assaulting the ears of passers-by with raucous music played on the tinniest of gramophones, stood an inferior version of Woolworth's – Marks and Spencer – giving no sign of the future style of the nationwide retailing organisation of the post-war years.

Lewis's Department Store.

By courtesy of Yorkshire Evening Post

23

Between Woolworth's and Marks and Spencer were plenty of shops, including two of the city's main department stores. Mathias Robinson on one corner was a superior establishment, one of the 'posh' shops. On the opposite corner was Hitchen's, a very boring store which sold dresses, fabrics, fancy goods and haberdashery. It was a gloomy, overcrowded shop, old-fashioned down to the only exciting thing it had to offer. Invoices and money were put by the counter assistant into a container which was clipped to an overhead trigger mechanism. When pulled, the trigger released a powerful spring which shot the container along an overhead wire to a central glass windowed cabin housing a cashier, like a spider at the centre of a web of converging wires, who promptly dealt with the contents and sent the container back along the wire. It was a system which contrasted favourably with the rather sinister tubes serving a similar purpose in the more up-to-date stores. These gobbled the money containers with a horrible sucking noise and, on their return from some invisible office, vomited them into a wire mesh basket.

The most recent arrival on the retailing scene which had these awful pipes and other evidences of modernity was a branch of Lewis's chain store. It was one of the largest buildings in the city, seeming vast and boasting several storeys. There was nothing that you could not buy there – or so it appeared. Its customers were transported between floors, not only by express lifts, but they could also travel by escalator. These were entirely novel in Leeds and offered, without charge, a ride reminiscent of the fairground. They required, it is true, some judgement in the timing of when to get on or off and were therefore not well suited to the old, the infirm, or those suffering nervous temperaments. Once boarded, however, they carried the passenger aloft with widening vistas of the shop floor below, one cornucopia giving way to another. The ultimate in daring was to fight one's way down an ascending escalator – an anti-social practice which could result in ignominious ejection from the store.

Still within the central shopping area, but away from its most frequented streets, stood the main store of the Leeds Industrial Co-operative Society, strangely antiquated and depressing, selling solid, worthy clothes, built to last, but very dull in style. The strength of its attraction was the 'Divi' – the dividend on purchases, a small annual percentage credited to members proportionate to the total they had spent at the Co-op during the year. It was a significant element in the economics of working-class life, since for many it represented the only type of saving which their restricted budgets permitted. The Co-op store also had a lift, but it was a shaking, box-like affair which creaked up and down a central shaft, fully visible behind the lattice work of the protective metal mesh. Not even this, nor the dullness of its products could detach from the Co-op's role as a Temple of Thrift – a Smilesian institution in the city where the Reverend Samuel Smiles had first preached his earnest gospel of Self-Help to an audience of industrious artisans. As an organisation with branch stores throughout the city it offered most things that its members wanted, including milk and coal, culminating in its final service – undertaking. Even death paid a dividend.

As December approached – though still a long way ahead, the city's larger stores displayed the trappings of Christmas, early enough to bewilder a child. This was especially so for those clinging – all evidence to the contrary

24

and despite sceptical jeers from the more sophisticated contemporaries – to a belief in Santa Claus. How could it be that the dear old gentleman could simultaneously hold court in every store in town, having arrived, hot and sweaty beneath scarlet robes and whiskers in the warm sunshine of autumn, with never a reindeer or a snowflake in sight? How could he be also at the North Pole supervising all those industrious elves who were making the toys which were wanted? It required a major act of faith to reconcile these conflicts – or a huge capacity for self deception. A visit to one of these commercial Father Christmases imposed a further strain on faith. Part of the store where toys were sold, its usual display heavily augmented for Christmas, was converted into a 'Grotto'. Having paid a small sum, one entered a make-believe world usually centring on some nursery rhyme, a children's story or, more up-to-date, on the fantasy land of Walt Disney. Clockwork figures bowed and gyrated endlessly to appropriate music – "The Teddy Bears' Picnic" *ad nauseam*. There was an abundance of gnomes, supplied by the gardening department. None of it mattered very much to the quivering bundles of anticipation dragging their parents along towards the exit to meet Santa. Flanked by rather grubby little girls dressed as fairies, he listened all day to recitals of greed from rapacious children, to crescendos of rising expectations. Not surprisingly, he and his fairies often seemed rather peremptory in ridding themselves of their clients. At the end of each transaction, the supplicant was given a present from Santa's bag. Since it obviously was valued at less than the modest price of entry, the most impressive thing about it was the wrapping paper. Undoing it took long enough to take the recipient far enough away to render faint the cries of disappointment when at last Santa's mean streak was revealed.

The most disastrous flight of fancy, which did more to create healthy scepticism among the young, was the Co-op's 'Visit to Santaland'. Instead of the usual kind of Grotto presentation, it had been thought a good idea to simulate flight in a rocket. It was a brave, not to say, revolutionary idea. Children and their well intentioned gullible parents entered a door at one end of the box-like 'rocket', down each side of which was a row of seats – like an old-fashioned tram-car, which looked out on a rustic scene of blatant artificiality. When the seats were filled and the door closed, lights were flashed on and off and the whole contraption made to shake violently, while noises off imitated the imagined sound of a rocket. Simultaneously with these, an unseen hand cranked a handle causing the canvas, on which the rural scene was painted to move past the windows, creating an impression of movement. It was, alas, an unsteady hand which jerked the scenery in a most unconvincing manner, revealing a spasmodically unfolding panorama. The only sensation was that of sitting in an agitated box. No one but the most gullible, naïve child could have thought otherwise. Never can Santa have faced a less credulous audience than that released from the box when its convulsions ceased.

The Santas of the stores were the aristocrats of their mildly deceptive profession. As the season advanced, outside in the cold streets, placed strategically, were the lesser practitioners. Dismal and dispirited, their red cloaks threadbare and grubby, their whiskers ill-applied cotton wool on faces blue and pinched with cold, they were the negation of the Christmas spirit. They hawked trays containing cheap little toys or packets of balloons. "Jus' the thing fer the kiddies' stocking," they asserted. Not even the kiddies believed them. Sometimes, strained to breaking point by all these facsimile Santas, a child would accuse one of being a fake. To one such, a Santa near the market inclined an attentive ear. Gazing bleakly down at his tormentor, he gave him a pat on the head: "Why don' yer piss off, sonny?" he grated.

Aside from the big shops, Leeds had two special attractions for shoppers. Firstly, opening off Briggate, were the arcades, full of small shops and sheltered from the weather. Toy and sweet shops were abundant and in two of the arcades there were clocks with mechanical figures which, on the hour, asthmatically and arthritically, struck the time on a bell, while in the distance could be heard the deeply resonant notes of the Town Hall clock.

Secondly, there was the large municipal market building with stalls spilling over into the nearby streets. Within it and under cover were the opulent displays of the permanent stall holders – dozens of fruit and vegetable stalls, brilliantly coloured miracles of carefully piled produce – banks and pyramids of oranges and polished apples, mountains of sprouts and potatoes, loads of black and green grapes. The most shiny, the biggest and most flawless specimens were deceptively at the front of the pile. There were long rows of stalls specialising in meat, or game and poultry, or fish. Others offered cheap clothing and bales of fabric – dress materials, curtaining, plush and velvet. In the middle of it all was an unbelievably cluttered hardware shop, and at the bottom of the market, where there were stalls selling hot pies and peas, there was a special arcade where traders sold all kinds of pets. Outside the building, in an adjacent street, exposed to the weather, and lit by naphtha flares in the winter, were barrows tended by hawkers of all kinds, female as well as male, selling off cheaply inferior damaged produce. Their cries were, if anything, more strident than those of the stall holders inside, their line of patter abrasive, scabrous, witty and cajoling in turn, especially on the clothing and pottery stalls offering goods at 'knock-down' prices.

Helped by an assistant in a brown overall, who often acted as a foil, just as on the music hall the funny man often had a straight partner, the barker would display his goods to the waiting crowd. "I'm goin' to treat yer! Value? Yer've niver seen owt like this! A complete twenty-one piece tea service – genuine bone china, lady, none of yer earthenware rubbish 'ere; and this magnificent tea pot – guaranteed best Royal Crown! – 'ere lady, just 'ave a look – and this luvly 'and cut crystal vase! Now I'll tell yer wot I'm goin' to do. I'm selling the lot! – I can't be bothered with bits and pieces – only when they look like you lady! Oo's that with yer – yer 'usband? I'm only jokin', luv! Now where was I? Wot am I askin' fer this lot?" Pause, while the audience was invited to visit the nearest china shop, to see what they would charge. "Don't bother! Yer can trust me – I'll tell yer. Not a word of a lie – FIFTEEN POUND SEVEN AND SIX!!!" Another pause, followed by an appeal to the lady in front of the crowd. "You believe me, missus, don't yer? There I told yer! Now I'm not askin' fifteen pounds, I'm not askin' ten, I'm not askin' seven!" Another pause, followed by the adoption of a confidential manner. "'Ere! I'll tell yer wot I'll do. I'm goin' to treat yer. A Fiver the lot!! Now, who'll start me off at that?" Silence. Shuffling apathy on one side – eyes downcast, unwilling to meet his eyes; outrage on the other. Offended dignity, mixed with a thinly disguised contempt for the stinginess of the audience. Threats of smashing up the whole lot rather than letting it go for less than five pounds, sometimes actually carried out with a great lingering crash. And at the end, reconciliation achieved, somewhere about four pounds, ten shillings. Suddenly a hand in the crowd falters upward, quickly followed by another. Fred in the brown coat can't hand out the goods and take the money fast enough. And at last that lot is finished. The barker is in full control. "Now I know some of yer was disappointed. Well, I'll tell yer wot I'll do . . . " and so on. And at all the stalls, the sales techniques and their outcome were much the same. Purchasers went off with their bargains, happy to believe that they had got a lot for a little, counting what they had saved, in comparison with what their purchase would have cost in a proper shop. Had the dealer's protestations been true he would have been ruined on the spot. Incredibly, he was always there on Tuesdays and Saturdays and, so keen was he to give his wares away that on other days of the week he could be found in the markets of Dewsbury, Barnsley, Pontefract or any local market town.

On a piece of waste ground behind the official market and the neighbouring municipal slaughter house there was the Tatters' market. No stalls here, no barrows even: just collections of frowsty nth-hand clothing and piles of junk – old tools, piles of rusty nails and screws, half a dozen brass taps, a few old bits of wireless equipment, broken-down-looking old boots and shoes, laden bits of dirty-looking cloth on the ground – the lowest level of retailing possible. Here were disposed some of the items collected by going round the streets with a pony and cart shouting for rags and bones. No one seemed really interested in selling or buying. The whole scene was rooted in apathy, seeming to reflect the profoundly dull things for sale.

In all, it was a compact shopping area which ended abruptly on all sides. To the west, there was a sharp transition at Park Row to the business area of office blocks, banks and insurance companies – or Albion Street, if you discounted the short extension of Bond Street where the shops closed on Saturday afternoons as a mark of social superiority. On the south and east sides the area was bounded by Boar Lane and Vicar Lane and on the north side by the Headrow, with a short thrust northwards into New Briggate and Merrion Street.

This area contained not only the main shopping area of the city but also most of the entertainment which it could offer. In Upper Briggate, the Grand Theatre took all the touring companies on their way to and from the West End of London. It was, to give it its full title, the Grand Theatre and Opera House, visited by touring opera and ballet companies – but not too often. From time to time it was taken over by ambitious amateur operatic societies which flourished in the wealthier suburbs, but whose repertoire seemed never to go beyond the *Desert Song* or *Maid of the Mountains*. There seemed to be no higher praise than "he/she took his/her part well". Who would have thought that the cast had so many friends and relations? In Lands Lane, the Theatre Royal had a resident repertory company (two seats for the price of one on Monday). Or, at least, it did for most of the year. In fact, from Boxing Day to May the theatre was given over to pantomime. It was probably the

Briggate, showing the Fifty Shilling Tailor and Burton's, with horse-drawn cart, and tram.

By courtesy of Leeds Leisure services

longest running pantomime season in the North of England – probably in the whole of the British Isles – probably the whole world!

Also in Briggate was the Empire, presenting what was known as "Variety" – a latter day extension of the music-hall tradition. All the familiar comic turns of the day played the Empire, supported by all kinds of performers – jugglers, acrobats, dancers, magicians, trapeze artists, animal trainers, singers, pianists, all had their names in the two evening papers, the *Post* and the *News* and on posters all over the city. The size of print was a measure of fame. In pubs nearby there were photographs of many acts, signed with a flamboyant flourish. The real representative of the old music-hall in Leeds was the City Varieties. Though it only seemed to feature the less well known acts, it was a cheaper and poorer version of the Empire. In comparison with other provincial towns, there was at least an adequate range of live entertainment available in Leeds, in fact twice as much as now, for a much increased population. There had been an additional theatre – the Hippodrome but that had been an early casualty of competition – it was converted into a cinema, the Rialto. One always thought of 'the pictures', 'pics', or 'the flicks', rather than the films.

The wireless played a very minor role in my life. Partly this was because of the prodigious amount of homework which was required, which took care of the time between tea and bedtime, when all the best programmes were broadcast. But more important was the absence of any feeling of the wireless as playing a central role in our lives. It had not been long since we had gathered at Uncle Herbert's house to hear a demonstration of his cat's whisker apparatus. We had maintained a respectful silence while he fiddled with the contraption with excitement, as it uttered howls and shrieks. Then at last, faintly through a lot of crackling, came the sound of a voice as from the grave. It faded quickly and defied all attempts at recapture, but for a few moments we had been sharing a moment of historical significance. I do not remember a word which this spectral voice uttered. This must have been in the late 1920s. Shortly afterwards we acquired a radio set. Cosser by brand, it came in two parts, the loudspeaker being detached from the cabinet. It imparted a hollow sound to the human voice, as though the speaker was in a cardboard box, and was prone to frequent attacks of extraneous noise against which the BBC fought a losing battle. This was followed by a Mullard and a Pye, by which time the wireless set had grown into a piece of furniture proclaiming its status as a household god. All this meant that it was about 1935 before listening to the radio seriously was possible in our household. I remember some of the dance bands of this time – Roy Fox, Sidney Lipton, Geraldo, Harry Roy, Jack Payne, Jack Hylton, Carol Gibbons, Henry Hall . . . The names come back so quickly and in such profusion that I wonder how I found time to listen to them all.

The cinema organ reached its apotheosis by having a resident organist at the BBC, Sandy Macpherson, and regular visits to the Tower Ballroom, Blackpool, to hear Reginald Dixon, or Reginald Fort or Robinson Cleaver direct from the Odeon, Hammersmith. The days of the electric cinema organ – "the mighty Wurlitzer" as it was often billed – like the days of the dance bands, with their serried ranks of brilliantined musicians performing with well-drilled precision, seemed to be durable and fated to go on for ever, just like the tram. If the BBC's programmes were not to one's liking there was always Radio Luxembourg, though it was tainted by being commercial radio and therefore not quite nice. I can recall some of the jingles used to advertise the products:

> "Hurrah for Beetox!
> What a delightful smell.
> The stuff that every self-respecting
> Grocer ought to sell."

and

> "Mine's a Minor
> The ten minute smoke
> For intelligent folk
> Nothing finer
> So why don't you try one of mine?"

went the cheerful ditty advertising De Reszke cigarettes. Or to round off the day:

> "We are the Ovalteenies,
> Happy girls and boys . . . "

For all my ability to recall the introductory jingles, for the life of me I can summon up no details of the programmes which they introduced. They remain isolated fragments upon which there is no basis to form any judgement of commercial radio. In fact, the whole of my recollections of wireless are equally fragmentary. Which is why I am so dismissive of it. It was pretty unmemorable.

A Leeds tram

By courtesy of Leeds Leisure Services

CHAPTER 4
Entertainment

Cinemas in the centre of town included the Scala, just off Briggate in Albion Place; the Tatler on Boar Lane, a small cinema specialising in presentations of the news, cartoons and eventually foreign films; the Tower and Assembly Rooms, both in Upper Briggate; and in City Square stood the Majestic. This cinema tried to compete with the between-film entertainment given by the organs of the Ritz and the Odeon, by featuring an orchestra – a larger version of the small ensembles which provided background music for clients having afternoon tea in the larger hotels. Both the Ritz and the Odeon were new arrivals in the 1930s. Belonging to chains which covered most big towns, they outshone their rivals. With their lavish décor, their acreage of gold paint,the thickness of their carpets, their palatial lavatories, the well-sprung comfort of their seats, but, above all, in their cathedral-like dimensions, they introduced a new and much needed dimension of luxury into cinema-going in Leeds. The centrally located cinemas, particularly the Odeon, Ritz and Majestic, were quick to show the latest films which had been announced and reviewed in the national newspapers. Visits to them were disturbing as well as a special treat. They aroused feelings of discontent with, even contempt for, the smaller, humbler suburban cinemas which would not show the latest films until weeks, even months, after they they had been shown in the city.

For a boy in the 1930s the city's many public houses had no interest. From time to time a door swung open onto the street, emitting a sudden blast of noise and smell of drink mixed with tobacco smoke – a sort of social belch to remind the godly, sober and under-age that sin and wickedness were abroad. Inevitably, around closing time, on the pavement outside the pubs, were men and women, continuing arguments begun inside, or earnestly engaged in some transaction. There were many breweries in Leeds owning public houses selling only their own products. The most numerous and popular belonged to Joshua Tetley, the smell of whose brewing was evident on the way into town, as the tram clattered along Meadow Lane, past the much smaller brewery, Mcquatt's. Then there were the pubs belonging to the Tadcaster breweries, John Smith and Sam Smith, and other out of town breweries, Ramsden, Bentley and Hammond. Near the centre of the city the Melbourne Brewery added its contribution, and there were the suburban breweries of Hemingway and Kirkstall. These were all firms of brewers located within a radius of twenty miles of Leeds. In addition, there were pubs which belonged to the mammoth breweries of Burton-on-Trent – Bass, Ind Coope, Allsop – and to the Scottish brewers, Younger. A few public houses were outside these networks and brewed their own beer in small back-yard brewhouses – a vestige of a tradition which had still been strong locally fifty years before. Amongst others, there were the 'Crystal Spring' near St. James' Hospital, the 'Lamb and Flag' out at Seacroft, and, probably the best known, the 'Malt Shovel' in Armley, its owner also being the proprietor of a small bus company. By comparison with the much more restricted range of choice now available, as a result of mergers between brewers, the beer drinker in Leeds in the 1930s faced an almost bewildering array of products.

Otherwise, Leeds offered little entertainment aside from sporting activities, which, anyway, were suburban rather than centrally located. The Town Hall had a large concert hall with mottoes around the frieze, erased by a later, more self-conscious generation, but happily restored, perhaps in deference to the Victorians who proudly displayed them, as a kind of assertion of virtues. They read: 'Honesty is the Best Policy' and 'Weave Truth With Trust', for example, and *Labor Vincit Omnia*. Here was held, in the winter months, a series of orchestral concerts, to say nothing of the Leeds Triennial Music Festival. And there were, around Christmas and Easter, performances of oratorios – the *Messiah* had to be performed at least once. Other favourites were *Judas Maccabaeus, The Creation, Elijah*. The hall could on occasion be transformed for a quite different audience – for professional boxing or all-in-wrestling, a relatively recent addition. Fights, concerts, oratorios, large political meetings were all outside the scope of boyhood interests, with one exception. The vivid posters advertising the all-in-wrestling performances at the Town Hall and Armley Swimming Baths carried not only pictures of the contestants, but brief biographical details. Of one, the public was informed: "He prays to Allah before he fights". He was known as 'Ali the Wicked'. Another wrestler was 'Scotland's Man Mountain'. Others had, it seemed, perfected various special holds – the 'Boston Crab', which sounded very unpleasant, the 'Whip' and various nautical sounding discomforts, the 'Nelson' or 'Half-Nelson', and, for good measure, the 'Japanese Stranglehold'. They were nearly all champions of some sort of area – the world, the empire, Europe, any continent, Britain, England, the North, the South, the Midlands, Yorkshire. Never seeing them in the flesh, let alone demonstrating their expertise, one nevertheless acquired a familiarity with them from their posters. They were part of a fantasy world which could never have been matched in reality.

What happened if, instead of catching a tram bound for the city, one went in the opposite direction? Not a great deal. On the left were the long parallel rows of houses each with one or two shops at the end facing the main road. They were mainly various kinds of food retailers, including fish and chip shops which offered bliss in used newspaper. A twopenny fish (my recollection is that the fish was cod, rather than the ubiquitous haddock of today) and a penn'orth [a penny's worth] of chips, well sprinkled with vinegar and salt. On request, a generous helping of crisps was added, free of charge. On the right was a walled field, known as The Manor, again, with what relevance to a long vanished past one doesn't know. On looking down from here, Elland Road Football Ground was visible. It was only a short

Elland Road Football Ground, with the back-to-back housing in the distance.

By courtesy of Leeds Leisure Services

Elland Road showing tramlines and overhead lines.

By courtesy of Leeds Leisure Services

distance down, reached by going along the ginnel [alley] which started alongside The Manor, to sample once every two weeks its assortment of pain and pleasure. The Leeds United team in those days reputedly had the best half-back line in England, but somehow never managed to achieve distinction, were never league champions and never won the F.A. Cup, but seemed content with mediocrity. Still, each new season brought hope that this time it would be different.

Most of the accommodation on the football ground was fully exposed to the weather, though there was a miserable wooden stand for those who could afford to sit under cover and another, even worse, behind the goal at the Elland Road end, known as 'The Scratching Shed', presumably for the same reason that certain cinemas were known as 'The Fleapit' or 'The Bug Hutch'. One of the best informed critics of the game and of the individual performances of the players was my grandfather, who, having walked to the ground, entered free of charge when the gates were opened at three-quarter time, surveyed the dying minutes of the game from the top of the terracing, and walked home again. Somehow, he managed to acquire a knowledge of the whole match as good as those who had been present throughout.

There were no restrictions on the size of the crowd, so that, when the club was doing well and local enthusiasm was inflamed, the ground was so tightly packed that, once installed in some vantage point, it was impossible to get out – the only movement was that imposed by the surge of the crowd which swept individuals with it. At the end of the match one could see the puddles of the incontinent – a rolled-up newspaper used as a funnel came in handy. The urinals were pretty dreadful anyway. There was no violence. There was no mass chanting of rehearsed obscenities, or more innocent, but equally mindless, snatches of popular songs. There was no terrorising of the inhabitants of streets which had the misfortune to be on the way to the ground. The scoring of goals was not the occasion for a disproportionate display of mass hysteria by the players in particular, or by the crowd in general.

The players themselves wore long baggy shorts, club jerseys in appropriate colours – a kind of livery – thick woollen socks, beneath which were protective shin pads, grotesquely distorting the shape of their legs. Their boots were worthy of the name and were laced up to the ankle. The ball was not coloured white or orange so that its visibility to the spectators was enhanced. It was made of brown leather. Since there were no floodlights, a game in mid-winter, even with an early start in the afternoon, would end in near farce with the ball virtually invisible in the gathering dusk. In the absence of smoke control, it was likely that the low-lying pitch would be affected by fog on a windless day. With these conditions, not only was the ball invisible but, for those at one end of the ground, so were the players at the opposite end. Should play be concentrated there, the only clue as to its progress was to try to interpret the noises being uttered by those who could see what was happening. A goal scored in these circumstances was greeted not by a full-throated spontaneous roar, but by a ragged shouting as the news passed rather like a forest fire around the waiting crowd.

Players favoured short, close-cropped hair, smooth and shining with brilliantine – or more likely the recently introduced Brylcreme – when they first trotted on to the pitch. As the game progressed, after heading the ball a few times, the immaculate hair style degenerated into a rat-tailed look. All the players received the same rate of pay which, though impressive as a weekly sum, which exceeded those received by the members of the watching crowd and supplemented by 'benefits' from time to time, was less than generous when related to the brevity of a player's career and the high risk of injury which he faced. They offered nothing which would, as later, enable the player to make his fortune. Many players at the end of their careers simply reverted to ordinary occupations. Some became shopkeepers. Quite a few, trading on the glamour which clung to them, became publicans. As a class, the players were not as histrionic as latterly. When injured they suffered stoically, concentrating less on their immediate pain, but on the longer term prospects of getting even, especially if the injury was the result of foul play – which many of them were. There were players who, if tackled on the half-way line, contrived by some miraculous means to fall in the opponent's penalty area with an appeal, which might result in the drama of a penalty. Another was so addicted to fouling that he achieved the distinction of being booed by his own supporters. Heroes or villains, stars of the game and lesser lights, who can now be recalled with difficulty, these baggy-trousered men worked cathartic miracles for the Saturday afternoon crowds, clad in their cloth caps, mufflers and dirty raincoats.

It was always easy to tell the result of a game by looking briefly at the tides of men pouring away from the ground. Were they animated, laughing, gesticulating and shouting to each other, or were they quiet, shocked and pallid, like an army in retreat? There were households in which wives and children waited uneasily for 'him' to come home: would it be smiles and extra Saturday pennies and "What's for tea then, luv?" – or scowls, gloom, a clip round the ear and "I'm off out then" as the door slammed?

A match dominated the week-end. Firstly and miraculously, by the time the crowd arrived back in the city centre, the news vendors were already selling Football Specials. In prose written under extreme pressure was an account of the game which they had just seen, their remembered experience encapsulated in clichés. It provided more material to be studied and argued about. The language used in the report on the game was standardised so that it required minimal thought. Referees were always "refs" who "brooked no interference" or "waved play on", unless they "had no hesitation in pointing to the spot". A moment of high drama was, awarding a penalty kick for an infringement, the nature of which was usually "hotly disputed". Goalkeepers were "goalies" or "custodians", making "diving saves" or seeing the ball "flash by their finger tips". Where? Into the rigging or net, of course. Wing-forwards were inevitably "tricky", so long as they were not "starved". Inside-forwards shared these characteristics; additionally they were "schemers", who either "split the defence wide open" or "carved through" the opposition. Centre-forwards "unleashed" shots which were always powerful and usually "first time" as well, a combination which was irresistible when "on the target". When possible, they "rounded" opposing centre-halves unless the response to their "bustling" or "robust" style of play was to find themselves "in a vice-like grip" imposed by a "stopper centre-half". Tackles were of two kinds – "stiff" or "crushing" – especially when inflicted by stopper-centre-halves or full-backs who were "cool under pressure" or "badly rattled by the home team's tactics", that is, were getting more stiff tackles than they were doling out. Otherwise, tackles were "fair" or even "perfectly fair", meaning that the player tackled could limp away. "Stiff" tackles meant that the recipient was probably carried off the field. The most severe punishment was to send off the offender which meant that his team was reduced by one player for the rest of the game. Next in severity was the award of a penalty, which exceeded sending off, if not in consequences, then in sheer drama, which silenced the crowd as the player nominated to take it stepped up to the spot and the goalkeeper froze into immobility, as laid down by the rules of the game. The episode might end in anti-climax, with a muffed attempt, the ball "cannoned off the woodwork", "hit the upright", "crashed against the crossbar" or "flew harmlessly" past crossbar or upright. A truly struck shot "sent the goalie the wrong way" or otherwise eluded "the hapless custodian" ,in which case the ball "ended up in the back of the net". "Moves" took place down the right or left flank", the "opposition" was "bewildered", as well it might have been, after the machinations of those scheming inside men and the tricks of those wingers.

The phrases, repeated every week of the season by all sports papers all over the country and again for good measure by the sports writers in the Sunday papers, were used over and over again in countless discussions and arguments which carried the game forward on a tide of beer, far into Saturday night. Sunday, with its journalistic contribution, guaranteed a resumption. The arguments were of two main sorts. There were those which raged around incidents or tactics in the game just played and particular player's performances in it. Then there were those which were more mellow and reflective, shot through with nostalgia, full of appeals to history and recounted memories of long distant games and players recalled briefly from oblivion. Sometimes such arguments reached an impasse from which they could only be rescued by appeal to the columns of the local sporting paper.

It was a humble form of scholarship, which required extensive and detailed knowledge of the game to clothe emotions and passions which, for many otherwise meek and inarticulate men, could only be aroused as they re-lived those fortnightly flashes of drama which punctuated their drab lives.

What other sights were there on the short journey to the tram terminus? There was a black but otherwise unmemorable Parish Church surrounded by soot-stained gravestones; the Wesley Street chapel; a branch of the Co-op and the Beeston Picture House, one of several within easy walking distance.

As an added attraction to what was showing on the screen, the Picture House had on Friday and Saturday nights an organ for the audience's entertainment during the intervals, while it browsed and munched through choc ices and sweets. It was not an organ like those at the Odeon or Ritz, which rose from beneath the floor in a blaze of coloured lights and a welter of music, as the resident organist played a much decorated and embellished version of his signature tune. The Beeston Picture House organ simply stood waiting at the bottom of the stalls, silent and unilluminated. In imitation of the masters of the craft who were to be heard on the wireless, Joseph Lee had his own signature tune, which he foolishly played at the end, rather than, as was customary, at the start of his recital. It was the optimistic song *Happy Days Are Here Again*. Unfortunately, this often conflicted with the opening music of the first film on the programme, so that he was drowned out, or lost the drift of his own music, petering out uncertainly. Sometimes he responded with a defiant gesture of crashing chords and musical curlicues. His performances were always high risk occasions. There might be trouble from the underprivileged and musically unappreciative part of the audience who filled the front rows and were nearest to him. There were, all too audible, the noises made by late arrivals treading heavily down the thinly carpeted floor of the gangway, this being followed by tip-up seats crashing back into place. There were the audible transactions between customers and those usherettes who sold refreshments, and the asthmatic wheezes of the hand-spray used to mask other less agreeable smells in antiseptic fumes. These were strong enough to make those within range cough, thus adding to the noises with which Mr. Lee had to contend. Of course, he had his small moments of triumph when the audience sang in response to some familiar tune. Usually he concluded to generous applause, which he acknowledged with a dignified wave and an incline of his well-oiled head. Not for him the antics of the organist at the Odeon, who waved with both hands, having first swung round on his seat as the spotlight shone on his white suit and flashing teeth.

None of the cinemas within ten or fifteen minutes walk could boast a similar attraction. Probably because of the disinfectant spray, the Beeston Picture House was not known as a fleapit, which was more than could be said of most of its competitors. The manager of the Crescent graced one's homeward departure by wearing evening dress. The Crescent also had dancing for anyone so inclined, which gave it an advantage over its rivals, and used the word "ballroom" in its advertisements, which sought to place it in a higher social bracket than them and was on an equal footing in the provision of two or three rows of 'snogging-seats' at the back of the hall. These were double seats in which couples wrapped themselves round each other, oblivious to what was going on on the screen, which was understandable, where the smallness of the houses made impossible any exchange of intimacies and the district was generally bereft of places to be apart. It had its drawbacks. Sitting for three hours with an unrequited erection was likely to precipitate a severe case of 'lover's nuts' for which an illiberal society left one totally unprepared in an area where things could go drastically wrong. Oh! the times one spent anxiously examining one's tackle by torchlight in bed. But what was one looking for?

Not far along the route from the cinema, Beeston took on the undoubted appearance of a village rather than a suburb. There were no longer acres of streets laid out in geometric precision. Instead, the main road was flanked by tall old trees and houses, set randomly in gardens, all of which were laid out differently. Some of these houses were grouped together and were name-plated as 'Folds' and added to the sense of rurality created by a few stone-walled fields and paddocks. It has all been destroyed.

At the terminus stood Beeston National School which looked like a village school. On some evenings it served as a branch of the public library system and the classrooms in which the cupboards of books were kept smelled of hyacinths in spring time, quite unlike our malodorous rooms with their mixed smells of human occupation. Ante-dating the great red brick barns built to house the Victorian masses for whom the Forster Education Act of 1870 catered, and differing from them in style, the school still functions. Opposite the school was the 'Railway Tavern' which has now been replaced by the 'Whistle Stop'. The 'Railway Tavern' was built for the convenience of passengers of the station just down the hill, through which the London-bound expresses hurtled. It had stone-flagged, uneven floors and small cosy rooms, in which conspiring could take place, with labels on the doors – "Taproom", "Snug", "Jug and Bottle", where people waited for their jugs to be filled. The provision of rooms meant that one could drink privately without being seen by anyone with a bit of authority to wield.

By courtesy of Yorkshire Evening Post

The Majestic Cinema.

CHAPTER 5

Outdoors

From the tram terminus there was a view from the spur on which the village stood, across the valley carved between the rhubarb-growing fields by the noxious beck – with its waters polluted to a black colour by dyes – to the small mill town of Morley, and other industrial villages like Drighlington and Farnley, which were still separate entities. It was a strange landscape, recalling itself to mind, not as on a fine day, but as seen on a grey afternoon in winter. There were scattered mills from whose chimneys black smoke trailed and a few derelict coal mines with head-stocks and the clusters of pit-head offices in various stages of decay. And rows of workers' houses which bore no meaningful relationship to each other, but all displayed the same spirit of meanness in matters of space, as though they were located in some central urban street in one of the new manufacturing towns, where space was at a premium and an economic rationale could be invoked to explain their overcrowding. Here, they were set down amidst land for which there was little alternative use, but they were still cramped and of back-to-back construction like the rows of houses that the tram lurched through every day in Leeds.

The main crop which grew here was rhubarb. Distinctive low sheds, all light excluded, were forcing sheds in which grew a crop which hit the market in January. Bright pink, with yellow foliage, it was in such demand that an express train left Leeds at night to deliver its crop to the London market. It was altogether smaller than the field or garden-grown variety which came later in the year. This was thicker and coarser, green and red and had large green leaves. Eaten raw, it was juicy and sharply acid and had highly purgative properties. It was known as 'tusky'.

Most of the Leeds suburbs still had similar villages as their nuclei, increasingly engulfed by the city's expansion, superimposed on whatever more local dynamics of growth were at work. These villages had, until the early nineteenth century, or later, been quite distinct, dominated by agriculture, or like Armley or Bramley, Holbeck or Beeston itself, a mixture of agriculture and domestically organised woollen production. On the eastern side of the city, Seacroft was still a completely separate village, though located within the city boundary, a pleasing collection of cottages around a village green and only accessible from a distant tram terminus at Crossgates. In spring, one walked to it along a lane fragrant with may blossom.

The town of Morley, clearly visible across the valley from Beeston, was a separate municipality with its own Town Hall and Mayor. It was served, however, by Leeds trams which groaned slowly up the hill to it from the valley bottom. It was a woollen manfacturing town, specialising, like Batley and Dewsbury, to the west, in producing cheap, low quality cloths in which virgin wool was mixed with mungo and shoddy. These were one of the end products of the activities of the rag-and-bone man. The wool rags and old clothes which the rag-and-bone men collected for a small price from the householder all found their way to the 'Heavy Woollen District'. There they were ground into a fibrous mass which, when cleaned, was blended in varying degrees with new wool. The whole world sent its rags there, to be sold at the Dewsbury Rag Auctions – a bizarre and smelly trade. Even the worn-out uniforms of the Leeds tram crews were collected and sent to the Heavy Woollen District to be ground up, prior to being incorporated in new cloth. There was no telling how many times woollen garments might have been worn, discarded, ground up, and re-manufactured. Nor was this the last word of an economising spirit. The dust from grinding, a mixture of wool fibres too short for further use in cloth manufacture and the dirt falling from the mixture being ground, was collected and left outdoors to rot, until it became a rich source of organic manure upon which plant life throve. This was said to be the reason for the location of the rhubarb cultivation which was so highly concentrated in the same area.

A field behind the Beeston Picture House every autumn was the venue of Beeston Feast. Compared with the major Feasts held yearly in the city, and, notably, Hunslet, Holbeck, Armley and Woodhouse, which were all held on the 'Moors' in their respective suburbs, Beeston Feast was a matter for derision. It did have its small attractions, making do with one roundabout instead of twenty. Everything else was proportionately scaled down, except the Herculean athletics of the Performing Fleas, the Gigantic Rat and, of course,the Fat Lady. The coconuts were as impervious to a direct hit as elsewhere and the brandy snap, toffee apples and candy floss just as indigestible. It was equally easy to lose one's all on the deceptively simple penny-rolling stalls, retiring sick with remorse, pale and trembling at the loss of sixpence. Equally easy to win was a virtually useless prize, at one of the various games of chance or modest skill – throwing flat wooden rings on to pegs, or tennis balls into gold-fish bowls, each containing a small fish as a prize, darts at playing cards, or firing at moving targets with ancient air guns. Beeston Feast also offered, like the other feasts, the oportunity to bid for glory by taking on one of the pros at 'Professor' Hughes' Boxing Academy.

The professionals lined up on a platform outside the canvas booth and glowered out at the crowd intimidatingly. They were wrapped in seedy dressing gowns and wore impressive laced-up boots. They were an unprepossessing bunch of thugs – bent noses, cauliflower ears and eyebrows swollen with scar tissue. Hair greased flatly against their heads, blinking in the light of naphtha flares, they waited brooding and menacing for someone, anyone in the crowd to offer a challenge as the 'Professsor' tried to whip up the fighting spirit which was lurking in his audience.

"Five Pounds! One whole Fiver! Five smackers and 'arf the collection to anyone as can stand for three three-minute rounds with one of my boys." This was, before the war, a considerable sum. Five pounds a week was more than anyone in the audience was likely to be earning. "He is a five pound a week man" was a phrase used to describe someone who was doing well in the prevailing economic gloom. With this lavish inducement, a challenge was usually forthcoming, several on a good night. Some of the hopefuls were known to the crowd as having a useful reputation. They toured round the Feasts, making beer-money. Mostly, the challengers were gullible youths, or notorious public house brawlers who relied on brute strength and luck to see them through. Some were already 'pot valiant', some drunk with the prospect of success. A few were, frankly, part of a put-up job. From the back of the crowd, they hurled insults intended to 'needle' one of the 'Professor's' boys. They fooled some of the crowd into believing in the imminence of, if not a fight to the death, then a contest of terrible ferocity – "'Im! 'im at the end, wi't short back an' sides. 'Im wot looks like a bleedin' gorilla. Couldn't fight 'is way out of a paper bag. I'd fight 'im any day with one 'and tied!" The object of the challenge generally smiled thinly back – a smile lacking warmth, or simply blinked a few times, otherwise maintaining his bleak stare at the crowd. He might, on occasion, make a show of offended professional pride and make to leap off his platform and finish off his tormentor on the spot. He was, of course, restrained by his colleagues and 'Professor' Hughes, who, least of all, wanted a free-for-all.

And so, thrilling in anticipation, we paid our entrance fee and trooped in, standing around the raised ring. One by one the challengers, stripped to the waist, wearing their ordinary trousers and perhaps a pair of plimsolls, were disposed of by the resident team. Flailing away desperately and ineffectually, most of the novices were soon puffing and blowing mightily. They were allowed a brief period of tolerance. The challenger might even be lulled into an illusion of impending victory. His opponent would allow a few blows to alight in some inconsequential part of his body, feigning distress, buckling at the knees and covering his face in an attempt to avoid further punishment. At the end of the round he tottered back to his corner,where his seconds worked hard to revive him, waving a grubby towel in his face and taking from a bottle mouthfuls of cold water, which they blew in his face. Meanwhile, in the opposing corner, our hero, encouraged by his supporters, waited impatiently for the next round and victory. Somehow, his opponent recovered and became more purposeful. Blows which had previously missed their target began to land with jolting effect. Some were lower than they should have been, bringing a howl of rage from the challenger's supporters and a finger wagging admonition from the referee, protests of injured innocence from the offender, followed by an act of contrition and a sporting gesture as gloves were touched. All too late and irrelevant for the pained and damaged challenger. His end was near and shortly he would be knocked out or retired by the referee. "A hand for the gallant loser," 'Professor' Hughes would cry and, as a consolation, a share of the proceeds obtained by passing round the hat.

The quality of acting in the 'grudge' fights was not high. There was a lot of grimacing and grunting and much wobbling and staggering, even pleas for mercy in the face of such unendurable suffering. On one occasion, both fighters ended up on their backs having delivered simultaneous knock-out blows. The audience was in hysterics. Occasionally, there must have been glimpses of the real thing. How otherwise had the pros acquired their rugged looks? Were any of them on the way up? Could any one of these 'boys' be a future champion? It was surely not unknown. All I can say is that I never heard of it.

If Beeston Feast was a small affair, there was no doubt about the impressiveness of the others, the nearest being on Holbeck and Hunslet Moors, which were not moors at all. No heather or gorse or whin had ever grown on them. They were open spaces, bequeathed for public recreation, set in the middle of old industrial suburbs. Flanked by houses, pubs and works, their surface consisted of grit and finely ground cinders. In winter they were marked out for football. In summer they did duty as cricket pitches, with piles of discarded clothing for wickets. No flannelled fooling here. The surface of the Moors was too uneven for the use of a proper hard cricket ball. If delivered at all fast, shooting off the surface at unpredictable angles, it would have crippled the batsman sooner or later. Instead, a thankful municipality, wishing to encourage wholesome sport among the lower orders, had laid down concrete pitches. On these the ball behaved more reliably, but was still very responsive to speed, flying off the hard surface at a fast pace. It was fashionable for aspiring bowlers – for this was the age of Larwood and Voce – to run for prodigious distances up to the wicket, acquiring momentum before sending down their delivery. Some overdid this. Towards the end of their over they were so exhausted that they lacked the strength to offer anything other than the slowest of deliveries. "It's me slower one," they panted, wincing as the batsman contemptuously smote the ball into the far distance. Cricket was much less damaging to play on the Moors than football. A fall on that abrasive surface yielded unpleasant wounds filled with black grit which, if not removed, left a blueish scar, like those visible on coalminers.

Annually, however, the moors were covered with the gaudy paraphernalia of their feasts: roundabouts galore, swings, dodgem cars, whips, speedways, walls of death, chair-o-planes, great elephantine steam boats – all those devices on which people spent money to be made to feel, but not actually be, sick or, as on the steamboats, terrified, as they felt gripped by uncontrollable forces likely to go beyond the point of endurance. The gentlest, most sedate and pleasurable of the rides was the ordinary roundabout of steeds with great flaring nostrils, plunging up and down as the clockwork figures danced to the music of the organ and the ride became faster, but still not so fast as to require the assumption of an air of nonchalance, as on the more violent rides. Nor did they inspire fears of mechanical failure, like the chair-o-planes, which, with the power of centrifugal force, hurled one's chair-seat out above the faces in the crowd.

The Feasts could be heard a long way off, the mixture of noises distorted by distance, carrying on the still air of autumn nights, the sky illuminated by the glow of their lights. And then, after a few nights, it was all over for a year. The lumbering waggons, into which the amusements and side shows were packed, moved on to the next venue, leaving the Moor empty and looking even more desolate than its natural state warranted. With them went the brightly painted caravans of the show people – the proprietors of the various rides, fortune tellers, the owners of amusement arcades, rifle ranges, coconut shies, boxing booths, freak shows, menageries, halls of mirrors – red of face and loud of voice, dedicated to parting the gullible from their money. Some were reputed to be rich, as the florid decoration of their caravans suggested and what could be done with chrome and plate glass confirmed. Many, however, looked poor and were mean in the stratagems which they used to cheat children out of their pennies.

There had been a time when the Feasts had deserved their name – occasions for much eating and drinking. Houses nearby were said to have been open for the entertainment of relations and friends before they went to the feasts. This aspect of the festivities seems to have disappeared by the 1930s, if, indeed, it had ever existed, other than as a feature of someone's imagination. It is an aspect of a Merrie England view of an idyllic and probably fictitious past.

The 'moors' were also the scene of the annual bonfire on November 5th or times of supposed national rejoicing, such as the Jubilee and the Coronation. They were also used for the holding of large political meetings. One such occasion was the holding on Holbeck Moor of a rally by the British Union of Fascists, the blackshirts as they were known, led by Sir Oswald Mosley. The blackshirts wore quasi-military uniforms, jackboots and Sam Browne belts and appealed to the lowest common denominator, with a line in strident anti-semitism. They sought to introduce a new and alien style to British politics. A large crowd did assemble, dominated by men wearing cloth caps, mufflers and seedy-looking raincoats. Many were, or had recently been, unemployed. Most of the rest were in poorly paid, precarious jobs and lived in the mean streets of that part of Leeds. Was this strange figure perhaps a potential saviour from the hard times with which they were familiar ?

Mosley was to address the crowd from the back of a lorry, surrounded by uniformed bodyguards, arms folded, scowling out at the crowd. Their leader lifted his arm in the Fascist salute and opened his mouth to harangue the crowd. Through the cold air a stone, popularly known with some exaggeration as "'arf a brick", described a graceful arc. It struck the leader on the head. What he might have said no one ever knew. Hands in pockets, the crowd dispersed, one member, no doubt, congratulating himself with the feeling of a job well done.

Distinct from the 'moors', which were little more than cinder wastes liberally sprinkled with dog turds, the Park had carefully tended lawns – not to be trodden on, well disciplined beds of flowers – not to be picked, a variety of trees – not to be climbed, intersected by paved paths – not to be run upon. There were shrubs, bowling greens, tennis courts, an old men's shelter and a bandstand. Both of these structures were in an eastern style, like miniature pagodas, for no good reason. There was not another building for miles with an eastern influence in what, after all, was a prosaic slice of society. Old men congregated in their shelter in bad weather, producing, with their thick twist, an atmosphere like the upper deck of a Number 5 tram. It must have shortened their lives. They played cards and dominoes. They argued and quarrelled and probably bored each other silly. Occasionally they had a talk by an outside speaker. They set the tone in the upper part of the Park, reinforced by the uniformed Park Keepers, who were in agreement with them that most of the world's troubles were caused by boys – especially small ones – who should be told to "gerrof out of it" on all encounters. Hence the number of prohibitions concerning park property and the general heavy atmosphere in the upper part of it. They were probably right to regard us as so many barbarians, beating on the gates of their dwellings and only kept under control by waving walking sticks and shouts of "Bugger off, you young sods." Faced with such unanimous hostility we left them alone.

The bandstand was bigger, and, of course, open, where the old men's shelter was enclosed in glass. It stood in an open space above the tennis courts, serving as a promenade or a space to put a deck chair, hired so that one could listen and relax while listening to the music. It was not a venue for the really famous bands of the north, like the Black Dyke Mills, or Yorkshire Copperworks, or Besses O'The Barn, but it attracted lesser-known bands maintained by pits and works in the area. On Wednesday and Sunday afternoons in summer, the park was enlivened by their performances. 'Ta ra ra ra ra Boom ching ching!' went the percussion and the brass made suitable noises. A crackling of polite applause followed each piece. The pennies rattled into the wooden collecting boxes. Dressed for the afternoon, those Beeston matrons who could find the time paraded together or separately with their perambulators on Wednesday afternoons. On Sundays they brought their husbands when there was a bigger crowd and generally a better band – more reliable in the resonance and stability of the trombone, euphonium and cornet solos, its timing crisper and more confident in its attack on the music, its uniforms more uniform.

Lower down the Park, below the tennis courts, it broadened out but became less cared for. There were wide areas of grass and more trees, but no flower beds and no problems about walking on the grass. There were balding football pitches and concrete cricket pitches of the same kind as those laid down on the 'moors'. Though it was forbidden, the trees were climbed, the bark on the tree trunks shiny from frequent contact with bodies. The shrubberies were criss-crossed with well worn secret paths and thickly populated with 'dens', when in summer the leaves of the bushes aided concealment, for whatever purpose. They were an underworld for small boys trying their first cigarette, who were probably sick as a result, and in whose secrecy awareness of some of the differences between the sexes were explored.

At intervals in the open spaces were large square blocks of stone. In summer they were used as wickets. Their true purpose was to provide crude platforms for speakers to harangue their fellow citizens from on a Sunday morning before opening time. Accordingly there were often several meetings going on at the same time, though they were well separated. One stone would be mounted by a Conservative, another by Labour, a third by a Communist, who clenched his fist in salute and addressed us as "comrades", which was very satisfying. Although this was, surprisingly, a Tory ward, any tendency to smugness on the part of the Tory speaker was soon dispelled by some pertinent heckling. Elsewhere, there was a meeting of the local branch of the B.U.F. [British Union of Fascists]. Not very numerous, even less humorous, they postured and looked threatening at any sign of an incipient heckle. Their speaker was harsh, strident and much given to knowing and heavy sarcasm. Nobody dared to ask a question and everyone looked glum.

But all these pockets of varying degrees of political belief were eclipsed by the arrival in the park of the Social Credit Party. They were a Canadian importation, big in Alberta, with an obscure message for non-Albertians, whose local interpreter was a master at one of the city's high schools and nicknamed "Tosh", suggesting that he had failed to hoodwink his pupils. First came the sound of the distant banging of a big drum, increasing in volume as Tosh and his supporters marched onto the park. Those in the Party wore green shirts and berets. It was a time when it was fashionable, on the fringes of British politics, to dress up in shirts whose colour had a deep ideological significance. Apart from Tosh and his drummer, there were only one or two wearing these. The drum was their only instrument and their only supporters were small boys and, in so far as they could keep up with the brisk pace set by the drummer, two or three old men. No one seemed to care very much about the message which Tosh tried to deliver. If social justice was sought, it would be by an alternative route to that offered by him. They did enliven Sunday morning, however, and, compared with the blackshirts, they seemed to be a benevolent, friendly amd harmless group.

There was usually a policeman strolling around. His services were never needed. The main characteristic of these audiences was apathy. At five minutes to twelve most of the men in the audience began a steady but purposeful saunter towards the gates. The pubs opened at twelve. No oratorical powers that they would meet at this humble level could detain them.

Rhubarb – 'Tusky' – growing in fields.
By courtesy of Leeds Leisure Services

46

CHAPTER 6

Games

The school stood by the side of the park on the opposite side to our street. It was a large red brick building, standing in a large concrete yard lined with substantial iron railings. As with other schools of this generation, it had been designed to segregate the sexes, to which end there was an entrance to the building with 'Boys' carved in the lintel, and another, labelled 'Girls' on the other end. The concrete yard was divided into two halves, one for each sex. They were released from school at different times. They entered at different times. Never were they present at the same time on any occasion. The boys inhabited the upper floor, the girls the lower floor. On fine days, with the windows open, the sound of singing sometimes drifted up to us. We giggled and sniggered. Otherwise, each half of the school ignored the other half. The upper age limit of the school was fourteen. Pupils entered it on leaving the infants' school at the age of eight, having until that age been regarded as too young to be imperilled by co-education.

It was a school in which the teachers placed great emphasis on winning scholarships to high school at the age of eleven. This was the aim, to which all else was inferior. It was one which was apparently approved by most parents, who reinforced the school's cramming with their own exhortations to 'do well', when the prize was a free place in a high school – usually the nearest, Cockburn, which was in Hunslet. The fathers were mostly semi-skilled or unskilled workers, often in the engineering trades which were badly depressed in Leeds. Quite a few were on the railways – footplate men, centred on what was known as 'the Plant', down in Holbeck – working very long and irregular hours, often away from home and subject to oppressive company rules. The footplate men were still working coal-fired engines, so that their work, particularly that of the firemen, was hot, dirty and tiring. Some parents were clerks, shop assistants, or worked in the textile or clothing factories. Mothers sometimes worked, especially as clothing factory 'hands'. One or two of the fathers were themselves schoolteachers – an intellectual aristocracy – adding their professional expertise to help their children's progress, so that they acted as pace-makers to the rest of us.

It would be easy, in retrospect, to rehearse the harmful pressures and the educationally narrow and socially warped attitudes which the domination of the examination system both reflected and produced. It would be impossible to measure the amount of damage done, not only to those who failed the all-important hurdle and were left behind in the race – or so it seemed at the time – social failures at the age of eleven. The process was harmful, also, to those who won a scholarship, though in ways which were less obvious, whilst the air resounded with their gratified cries.

The parents of the young and successful thrusters were not, on the whole, a well educated group, nor, as a group, were they articulate. There was no Parent-Teachers' Association to provide them with a forum. If they met their children's teacher at all it would be on unequal terms, for the teachers were persons of learning and authority. The parents' attitudes to education doubtless lacked breadth and humanity. They were materialistic, practical and rooted in common sense expressed in phrases like "I want my lad/lass to have opportunities I never had," or, "I want him/her to have a good, safe, steady job." Education was about jobs. By definition, the type of job most desired for their children was in an office, which was thought to epitomise the desired qualities. It would, moreover, not involve lifting heavy objects, or work in high temperatures, or danger, or any of the perils of working on the shopfloor. It was also the case that office workers were in less danger than shopfloor workers of being thrown out of work entirely, or put on short time when business was slack. There was, of course, a hierarchy of office jobs, with banking at its apex. Then came jobs in insurance offices. At about the same level were clerical jobs with the local authority. A large proportion of clerks in the rates office or in the recently opened Civic Hall must have been recruited from the local high school. The ultimate consideration of all such employment was, however, that it was – and the word slips grandly off the tongue – superannuated!

The workhouse by the side of the Number 5 tram route had succeeded in driving its message home. These parental stratagems were rendered misplaced by the economic effects of the Second World War. They were formulated in a world dominated by heavy and chronic unemployment and fear of falling into a waiting abyss of poverty. Who, in the 1930s, could have foreseen these changed conditions; whose forecasts of their children's future employment prospects have failed to incorporate the likelihood of them being unemployed at some time? Who can criticise those parents for seeking apparently low-risk jobs which were also dull and boring – and also poorly paid? In one major respect this generation of children already reflected a conscious decision on the part of their parents to limit the size of their families to one or two. Not for them the burden of unlimited pregnancies still found among the labouring poor who were seen to be notoriously feckless in this and other respects. Did not proof of this exist when one contemplated certain families where the mister only had to "hang his trousers on the bed end" to make his wife pregnant – as she put it – with a not wholly regretful face. She already could muster seven children and there was a lot of unfulfilled potential for increasing the number.

In Beeston, therefore, the school served as a channel on which was focused much striving for social improvement. It was thus seen as a proof of its success when, in the mid-1930s, its pupils won a record number of scholarships entitling them to attend the local high school. In addition, they had won some unprecedented scholarship to go to 'the Grammar School'. So remarkable was this achievement that the winners were assembled together with their class teachers, the headmaster and the local M.P. for a photograph in the local evening paper. To appreciate the full significance of this scholastic triumph, it must be realised that the Grammar School was not only an academic but a social peak – the Everest of the 11+ examination system in the city. Like so many of its kind it was anciently endowed. Its pupils were almost all fee paying. This ensured its social selectiveness. Academically it was assumed to have high standards, but it may be wondered if these were higher than, if as high as, the best of the city's high schools.

Another characteristic of the school by the Park was its indifferent sporting record, since so much energy went into academic cramming and striving. It was a rugby-playing school. Not, as we were to find, the gentleman's code of rugby ('rugger', as played at the Grammar School), but Rugby League, the working man's game, played by part-time professionals. The sporting interests of the school were, therefore, focused less on Leeds United at Elland Road but much more on the local Rugby League Club, Hunslet. Its shabby little ground was situated not far away at Parkside, in a wasteland of miserable looking allotments, pigeon lofts and rhubarb fields. A railway line passed along one side and as a background there was the elephantine bulk of the 'Middleton Alps', or, more properly, the slag heaps of Middleton Colliery. Hunslet was one of three such clubs in Leeds which was thus important in that limited area where rugby league is played – the West Riding, principally concentrated in the Aire and Calder valleys, Lancashire and the Cumberland coast. The loyalties of pupils at the school were, not surprisingly, divided. On the one hand, family traditions often dictated support for Leeds United, with father and uncles whose main topic of conversation centred on United games and players dating back before the First World War. On the other, Rugby League was the school game and familarity with its rules and conduct was assumed. This conflict was repeated when a boy went to the Grammar School. No one in the family had any knowledge of Rugby Union, or knew anyone who played it, or of the deep social chasm which separated players of the two codes.

One of the problems which limited enthusiasm for Rugby League as played at elementary school was that it was hardly a street game. A well executed tackle on the cobbles or asphalt would very likely result in more or less serious injury to both parties. To play rugby it was necessary to make an excursion to the lower half of the Park where there was grass to fall on. It was easier to stay in the street, kicking a football around. Nor were rugby players featured on the cigarette cards as, from time to time, were football players. As a result, our sporting figures were drawn from the gallery of soccer heroes, whose mantles we freely assumed.

The street, of course, dominated our winter activities. The Park closed at dusk, which in the depth of winter set in on the way home from school. As well as football and lamp post centred games, there were other essentially street games, many of which were seasonal. Hop-scotch was played mainly by girls and anyway did not seem to have much point. Also, in early spring, there was whip and top, requiring a smooth piece of pavement and the expenditure of great energy to furiously lash the spinning top, coloured with chalk to produce an attractive effect as it spun. The pavement was also a classic location for games played with marbles – locally 'tawse' – provided that it wasn't the variant known as 'nucks in' for which a hole in the ground was required. A whole world of economic activity centred on the game. Individual marbles not only changed hands as the fruits of victory, but by a process of keen bargaining. A range of types of marble existed, with a corresponding hierarchy of exchange values. Most prized were 'milkies' with swirling white inside them, and 'blood alleys', similar in design, but red. Next in order were the other, lesser prized colours – blues and greens and, occasionally, exotic purples and yellows. Of less account, but by no means negligible, were the marbles made of clear glass with thin multicloured stripes in their depths. Well below these came the small change of the marble world – the plain orb made out of frosted green glass. They acted as stoppers in old-fashioned lemonade bottles. Finally and despicably, there were 'stonks' made from coloured earthenware. Ownership of these marked one off as a social outcast.

Marbles were only one type of commodity in which trade was brisk amongst our budding entrepreneurs. The disposition to truck and barter was strong and extended to cigarette cards, postage stamps and magazines, which were the most popular items. All the major cigarette manufacturing companies issued cards with their packets of cigarettes, each company changing its theme from time to time. The cards were in sets of fifty, with an attractive picture on one side and supporting text on the reverse. Sometimes we collected portraits of fifty footballers, sometimes cricketers, famous motor cars, trains, aeroplanes, film stars. Or it might be pictures of wild flowers, or wild animals, or domestic dogs which inflamed our acquisitive lusts. There was a brisk trade in cards necessary to complete a set. To get them meant pestering anyone who smoked who could be approached with a request, "Got any cigarette cards, mister?" The other was by trading 'swaps', according to their scarcity: as it might be twelve other cards for Clark Gable, fifteen for Bette Davis. The real tycoons traded whole sets of cards held together by a rubber band and these too varied in desirability, like stocks and shares.

The whip and top season coincided with that for 'bowls', that is, running along the pavement – to the public danger – by the side of a circular iron hoop, which was guided by a thin iron rod with one end looped round the hoop. There were wooden hoops, propelled by a stick, but they were looked down on, as being for cissies – like sledges lacking iron runners. In any case, they did not create the fine ringing metallic noise of an iron hoop as it coursed along the pavement.

We were not great conker enthusiasts, though not wholly averse to playing. It seems to have been more of a rural pastime, or, at least, one requiring the presence of horse-chestnut trees, of which there was a local dearth. The supply of conkers was, therefore, small and irregular and it remained a minority sport. What we did have – involving the use of string – was an explosive device, consisting of a key with a hole in its shaft, which was tied to one end of the string. To the other was tied a nail, the sharp end of which fitted snugly into the hole in the key. A mixture of sulphur and saltpetre was inserted into this hole amd the nail end rammed in to secure it. The whole assembly was then swung on the loop of string and struck against a hard surface like a wall. If all went well, this produced a gratifying explosion. If not, then the result was an anti-climax, or a misplaced explosion, which in one case shattered a boy's hand. Needless to say, it was an unpopular pastime with parents.

There was, of course, the much more innocuous type of banger, consisting of a wad of newspaper, tied up hard on the end of a piece of string, and used as an offensive weapon, especially around the time of the municipal elections held in November. Roving the streets in small gangs we would find a victim. Cunningly failing to disclose our own party allegiance, we would demand a declaration of his: "Wot colour are yer?" we hectored, bangers poised. The reply, be it blue, red or yellow, was irrelevant. The victim was assaulted with bangers until, satisfied with our display of wit and force, we traipsed off into the night singing:

"Vote! Vote! Vote! For . . . (Whomever)
You can't vote for a better man!
(Whoever) is our man
And we'll have him if we can
And stuff old (his opponent) up the flue!"

Leeds Rugby Supporters Club

By courtesy of Yorkshire Evening Post

CHAPTER 7

Street Life

The formation of the streets and grouping of families in them imposed a curious kind of social rigidity. Not only was our street a separate territory but even our half of the street, as has been indicated, was divided between the older houses in the top half (mainly rented) and our new houses in the bottom half (mainly owner-occupied). Not for years did we really know anyone in the top half and then only one or two, to whom, I supppose, we felt rather superior. But segregation was not by any means a matter of pathetic social snobbery. The families living "round te back", lived in the houses backing on to ours, which were as closely comparable as any houses could be. Yet, for all we knew of them, they might have belonged to a different race, so remote were their owners. A difference of two or three streets meant transition into a wholly alien, and, at the level of childhood, often hostile territory. A dividing line like the Park or the main road at the top of our street, which separated the Parkfields from the Marleys and the Nosters, had almost the status of an international frontier. Nothing would induce us to venture into the Marleys – not even though the fish and chip shop serving them was reputed to be the best for miles around. We viewed the Marleys like timorous settlers facing territory occupied by renegade Apaches.

Partly, all this was because for children, at least, the street was not only the focus, under parental eyes, of activity and play but was regarded by us like animals regard their territory. We did not mark its boundaries by peeing on them, but we had a strong sense that it was ours and we viewed with hostility any trespass by children from other streets unless they were, perhaps, friends made at school and therefore enjoying diplomatic immunity. Our allegiance to a concept – the street – evoked in us the same kind of passionate and ill understood loyalty as, on a larger scale, membership of a nation state. Our small world, like that involving nations, had its diplomatic negotiations and intrigues, its alliances, détentes, treaties and, of course, wars.

Each street contained, more or less, a gang, the strength of which depended upon accidents of social composition which determined the number, ages and sex, but, above all, the degree of fierceness and propensity to terrorise, of the children who lived in it. The street gang next but one to ours, for example, had a reputation like those of Attila and his Huns, simply because it housed one family – the Gills – large in numbers and all of them boys, with one exception who was reputedly a girl. The upper half of the next street, however, was also formidable because of the Jaggers, half of whom were girls – or passed for such, like Miss Gill, though the male half were older and even fiercer. A coalition between the streets was equivalent in power to an alliance between Russia and China. A street with disproportionately large numbers of small children was of no account, having too many burdensome dependants – potential hostages, and certainly slow runners, incapable fighters and tellers of tales to parents. Its time would perhaps come in a few years.

Activity between gangs was at its height in the weeks before November 5th. At no time was conflict more likely than when, at stake, were the coveted prizes of fuel for the bonfire of Guy Fawkes night. Gathering this began back in late summer and extended over a wide area. Not only were the weaker street gangs dispossessed of their booty by the strong and rapacious as they dragged it through the streets, but, the nearer Bonfire night drew, the greater was the danger of night raiding parties. Unless proper vigilance was exercised, these could empty a whole garden-full of junk carefully gathered during the preceding weeks. Some families, living in houses with wash cellars, stored their timber under lock and key until it was ready to go on the fire.

Provided that these perils were overcome, with enough fuel at the end to make a worthwhile fire, then November 5th could be enjoyed as part of a limited, unspoken truce. To have insufficient wood to make a decent face-saving blaze in one's own street, could meet with a generous invitation to join another street's festivities. Once the fires had started, there was no more raiding, and, if the gang in one street, boasted a fire which blazed far into the night, then it was only to be expected, wasn't it? Surprisingly, at the end of all this activity most streets could brag that next morning their fire was still alight – the ultimate test of a good fire. Added evidence was the size of the scar burned into the street after the ashes and charred bed springs and other bits of metal had been cleared away with the sad remains of all the spent fireworks. November 6th was anti-climactic, and usually a grey day. The air smelt of smoke. A day or two afterwards there was a sudden outbreak of colds at school.

Had the motor-car made more impact on the neighbourhood it would not have been possible to have such fires in the streets. Hardly anybody owned a car. In the whole of our street – including the top half – and then only in the year before the war, only one family managed to buy a car and this was true in all the surrounding area. It was a new car. A Morris Minor. Black, shiny, and very small, its main purpose seemed to be to drive the few hundred yards to and from the garage where it was kept and the place in the street where it stood, opposite the window of its proud owner's house. He spent most of his evenings and weekends polishing it and standing back for long silent periods of admiration. So much love expended on an inanimate object gave rise to critical neighbourly comment. It was not unmixed with jealousy. With this one exception, even the cheapest of Fords, or the miniscule Austin Ruby Seven h.p. – into which, incredibly, it was possible to fit four adults – or the most minor of Morrisses, was beyond local economic aspirations.

Streets were, therefore, unimpeded by parked cars and rarely disturbed by passing traffic. Only streets which provided a short cut between two main roads experienced much disturbance. Not many people visiting our street owned cars. Friends and relations of those living there were equally as unlikely to have one.

Functionaries like the insurance men collected their premiums on foot. So did the District Nurse make her calls, carrying her black Gladstone bag. Even as dignified an official as the School Board man, who inquired into cases of absence from school and whose friendly manner concealed a sleeve full of capricious powers, walked the pavements in large, well-soled, shiny black boots. All the tradesmen who supplied us with goods came by horse and cart – the milkman, the coalman, the greengrocer. Miscellaneous traders like the Donkey Stone man and the chimney sweep, lurking unexpectedly under the striped awning of a converted ice-cream cart picked up cheaply, all used horses or ponies to draw their assorted vehicles. One of the few callers who arrived by car was The Doctor – or rather one of the doctors who visited the district. Cars, like telegrams, were therefore associated with bad news. This was confirmed on those occasions when our street witnessed a cavalcade of black cars. Not really witnessed, in the full sense of the word, for custom dictated that a funeral should be a rather furtive affair, with all curtains behind all windows in the street drawn as a mark of sympathy and respect. It was part of a lingering tradition by which men bared their heads and stood to attention, hat held against chest, as the cortège passed by. It was, of course, still possible to be served by an undertaker who clung to horse-drawn hearse and carriages for the mourners – altogether a much more solemn and stately affair, with the black horses tossing their plumed heads as the hearse rumbled over the setts on their way to the cemetery. Much more dignified than the internal combustion engine.

Those who came into the street by car or cart were far from exhausting its traffic. Beneath them in the social scale came various men who carried their wares in barrows. There were ice-cream sellers who pulled heavy barrows which belonged to one of several Italian families who dominated the trade until the appearance of the Walls' ice cream man. He wore a peaked cap and a jacket and pedalled a cumbersome tricycle to which was attached a large refrigerated box, with the slogan "Stop Me And Buy One" prominently displayed. The Italian firms sold ice-cream in cornets and wafers, the filling being scooped out of a barrel. The Walls' man's ice-cream came in paper packets and tubs, with strawberry as well as vanilla flavouring. He also sold 'Juicy Fruits' at a penny a time, triangular-shaped sticks of flavoured iced water of appropriate colours – for a halfpenny he would cut one in half. In winter the Italian carts were converted for the roasting of chestnuts in a little oven. Other vendors sold hot pies. All had distinctive cries, advertising their presence and bearing little resemblance to the product which they sold, but being a sort of strangled cry of pain which one came to identify with a particular vendor.

The economic traffic had added dimensions. With no conveyance of any kind, there were rag-and-bone men carrying their haul in a sack; newspaper sellers with heavy bags slung over one shoulder, always in a hurry and, like the rag-and-bonemen, loud with their cries. Their visits were punctual, in the early evening, but on occasions of great moment, they erupted onto the streets wth cries of "Speshul!", usually bringing news of some disaster, a colliery accident with heavy loss of life, a railway collision, or, once, the failure of H.M.S.Submarine "Thetis" to surface on the waters of Liverpool Bay. Their distant shouts would become more intelligible. Doors would open, throwing a beam of light into the street as people in solemn anticipation and pennies in hand waited for the bad news. It was a much more dramatic way of being informed than hearing the impersonal voice of a disembodied newsreader on the wireless.

There was also a steady stream of men selling things from heavy suitcases – assorted haberdashery, cheap scent and soap, stationery, kitchen gadgets and brushes for all imaginable purposes. Most claimed to be ex-servicemen. A few women came, mostly gypsies who sold badly made clothes pegs and dreadful paper flowers fixed on to privet stalks. Their real business was to tell fortunes, credited, as they popularly were, with special prophetic gifts.

Lastly, there were the street entertainers. Some only came once. Others were regular callers who had placed us on their roster. Mostly they sang – badly. So badly, sometimes, that they were given money to encourage them to inflict themselves on other streets. Others performed on an assortment of instruments: the violin, the cornet, the penny whistle, the accordion, and the spoons. Or, more humbly still, the bones – two lengths of beef shin bones, boiled, polished and rattled together, a pair in each hand and struck on various parts of the body, presumably for greater effect, more or less in time with the music. The violinists were often serious musicians who had played in a cinema or theatre orchestra and had been thrown out of work as cinemas changed over to organs, and theatres either closed altogether or dispensed with their orchestras as economic measures to help to meet the competition of the cinemas. They were shabby-genteel, with delicate fingers partly protected against the cold by cut-away woollen gloves. Occasionally we were visited by a one-man band whose performance was more memorable for its acrobatic qualities than the music, unlike those of the 'Tingle Airy' men, as they were called. These were players of barrel-organs hired from the same Italian families who ran the ice-cream trade. All the man did was set a dial to select a tune and then turn a handle and, out of this ugly contraption, came the most gorgeously decorated music, full of trills and arpeggios and possessing a unique quality of sound. Sometimes the organs were as decorated as the music they played, gaudily flowered and with an abundance of mirrors. Their repertoire consisted of tunes made popular during the First World War – *Keep the Home Fires Burning* and *It's a Long Way to Tipperary*, or old favourites like *Over the Waves.*

Memories of that war were very intrusive. Many of the street performers and door-to-door salesmen wore medals pinned to their jackets and some carried an autobiographical card in an attempt to harrow the reader with a tale of undeserved misfortune after distinguished military service, and the consequent sufferings of helpless and starving dependants. Some preferred the mute testimony of a missing limb. Some were blind and tapped their way down the street with a white stick, ever alert for the approach of a sympathetic donor. Occasionally, with terrifying effects on small children, men shambled down the middle of the street who were still suffering from shell-shock, face working hideously, limbs twitching and jerking out of control, emitting strange animal noises intended to be heard as a song. Though they probably received more money than any of the others, they would have got more had not some people been too frightened by their appearance.

In a class of their own, however, when it came to extracting contributions was the Darby and Joan team whose appearance and style would have melted the asphalt to tears. She was a little white-haired old lady, fragile and neatly dressed, shabby and threadbare but clean. He was also small and equally threadbare, but he held himself with dignity and acted towards her in a touchingly protective manner. They looked the epitome of the deserving poor. To regard them as distressed gentlefolk was perhaps too extreme. After all, would members of such a social category descend to begging in the streets?

As if their appearance were not enough, their act was wonderfully calculated to exact the maximum sympathy and tribute. They pushed an ancient perambulator in which was a gramophone with a tin trumpet-shaped horn. They had little music to offer but it was carefully chosen to achieve the maximum poignancy. *Home, Sweet Home, Silver Threads Amongst the Gold, Just a Song at Twilight* were their staples. Strong brutal men, devotees of all-in-wrestling, Rugby League and beer, notorious wife beaters, public house tearaways and potential child stranglers might resist one tune, but the second would see them choked with emotion, searching their pockets for money to give to the dear little old lady. Their visits round the streets were rare. Usually they favoured a pitch in the city centre on the corner of Commercial Street and Trinity Lane. Cynics said they were very wealthy, but this sort of thing is said about well-known beggars who at the end of the day are collected from an inconspicuous rendezvous by a chauffeur-driven Rolls.

'Cigarette Liz' inspired similar stories. She was a truly tatterdemalion figure, her face dark brown and weather-beaten, her hair dark and lank. All the clothing which she possessed she wore on her back, whatever the weather – various skirts and dresses, cardigans and jumpers and perhaps half a dozen coats. On her head one hat was piled on another with daring effect. Had she been able to wear more than one pair of shoes at once she would surely have done so. Invariably a cigarette drooped from her mouth and in her hand, or sticking out of one of her pockets, she carried a bottle of rum. It was hardly surprising that she attracted attention, walking along Vicar Lane or standing on the corner of Briggate. The sight of anyone staring at her, however, threw her into a rage. Foul mouthed and raucous, she would pursue her victim until he or she disappeared and would then stand, muttering valedictory curses until she decided to have a pull on her bottle. She was not said to be secretly rich. No Rolls Royce collected her at the end of the day. She was known to sleep on benches and in shop doorways. There was a rumour that she was the erring daughter of a county family, titled even, depending on the imagination of the teller, a victim of some unspecified tragedy which had brought her so low.

Not far from her most favoured haunts was another well-known character, whose pitch was on the pavement outside Holy Trinity on Boar

Lane. Hideously, grotesquely deformed, he could only propel his contorted body with the aid of two wooden blocks, one gripped in each hand. With the support of these he swung his body forward. His knees were level with his shoulders and his feet were the wrong way round. His crutch was almost on the floor. Pale-faced, with wire-framed spectacles, beak-nosed, wearing a cloth cap and muffler, he was delivered to his pitch in a morning and collected in the evening on a hand cart. There he remained with a waterproof cape for wet weather, a frightening spectacle to children or anyone at all squeamish. Neither he nor Cigarette Liz were ever seen other than in the city centre. We never saw them in our street. Otherwise, it was remarkable that in a dull, obscure suburban thoroughfare there should be so much extraneous life and incident.

The inhabitants of our street were quiet, hard-working and respectable, not given to flamboyant behaviour. Their ability to buy their own houses, invariably with the help of a mortgage, meant that they were a thrifty group, since all the wage-earners were semi-skilled and therefore modestly paid. They were sober: no drunken scenes or brawls disturbed our peace. Within the constraints imposed by the close proximity of the houses they kept as much as possible to themselves and yet contrived to be neighbourly. The men were much less evident than their wives. Out all day at work, there was little for them to do outside the house in the evening. The gardens were too small to require much care and too public to sit out in. It was the women who dominated the life of the street, making, maintaining or breaking friendships and enlisting the support of their families. They were much more frequently seen in their little gardens, sweeping, swilling the path, cleaning windows, scouring steps and window sills and hanging out the weekly washing. They always had time for 'call' or gossip, standing by the gate, arms akimbo. All of them were fanatically houseproud. Their new houses were kept immaculate and there was much competition, not only in degrees of cleanliness, but in material possessions. The decoration of the rooms, their floor coverings, the curtains, the furniture which they contained, the appearance of the gardens, were all objects of rivalry. There was, for example, the great leaded window craze.

For whatever reason, someone decided to replace their plain glass window panes with small panes of glass set in leaded frames. The earliest examples, expressed in small squares or diamond shapes, were a romantic imitation of what was thought to be Elizabethan or Jacobean styles, which to choose being a matter for agonised debate. Within a short time the windows of house after house were being altered, each owner managing to produce a variation on the original design, with pieces of coloured or beaten glass inserted. In some cases, a cheap version was used: strips of simulated metal were stuck on the orginal windows, which deceived nobody.

There followed the great wave of porches. The door of each house opened straight into the living-room, with no hallway, making it as draughty as a tree. An attempt was made in most houses to mitigate this unwanted ventilation by hanging a heavy plush curtain over the inside of the door. It was suspended from a horizontal pole so that the curtain could be moved off the door during the day. It was not a very effective device, but the structure of the house would have defeated any attempt at draught exclusion. Even if the house door could be blocked, there remained a gale of cold air sweeping down the staircase, straight across the living-room floor and up the chimney. The scullery door also contributed to the draught-induced discomfort. One lived in a windy vicious circle. The bigger the fire burning in the grate, the fiercer blew the draughts to feed it. The result was to be simultaneously roasted in front and frozen in the back. One attempt to reduce the severity of the problem was to build a wooden and glass porch which would shelter the house door and serve as a kind of lobby. In summer one could sit at one's ease, sheltered from the breeze. After one porch appeared others quickly followed – no two alike, of course – just to show that imitation was tempered by individuality.

The whiteness of the weekly wash was another way of expresssing competitiveness. Another was the race to be the first to hang the washing on the line – a display of moral virtue reinforcing that of cleanliness. Part of the social dynamic which actuated the community of the street was simply 'keeping up with the Joneses'. It evoked tooth-gnashing jealousies every bit as fierce as those in wealthier sections of society. It was, however, mitigated by a sense of self-ridicule, of mockery of excessive pretensions. Four streets away, in another row of back-to-back houses, lived someone posssessing baronial aspirations. On either side of his front gate he installed, on stone plinths, a pair of stone balls appropriate to a stately home. It was too much. No one copied this grandiloquent gesture which remained unique and the object of much sly ribaldry, based on the obvious symbolism

The embellishment of the house, already being purchased on a mortgage, was evidence not only of thrift, but also of steady habits to be able to keep up the regular instalments. It also required as an essential basis a job sufficiently secure and free from the danger of unemployment and short-time working in the eyes of building society officials that they would sanction a loan. In an economic sense, therefore, the people in the street were a self-elected élite. Though they were members of the working class by any standard, they were lucky to have jobs in the mid-1930s. Leeds, having varied industries, never experienced the extremes of unemployment on a scale known in areas like the North East or South Wales where the collapse of a single dominant local industry was wholly disastrous. Nevertheless, there was enough unemployment in the city, especially in the engineering trades, to make the fear of dismissal ever present for those in work. From time to time, one would become aware that in some household the head was 'on the dole'. The effects of this were often diminished by the wife having a job in the clothing industry, or by the wages of older children. In general, however, it was not a marked feature of life in our half of the street, though it was more apparent in the top half.

Even in our half there was not much of a margin left over, once basic needs had been met. The weekly joint which appeared hot on the table on Sunday and cold on Monday had to undergo various economical transformations before the bare bone could be thrown away. Minced, it appeared as rissoles on Tuesday; the remaining bits of meat and gristle clinging to the bone were the basis of Wednesday's stew. The competitive spirit was modest enough and no one displayed the trappings of conspicuous consumption.

CHAPTER 8

Holidays

Some families were able to get away for a holiday by the sea. This was what mattered most, no country holidays for them. And seaside did not mean a secluded cove where the North York Moors swept down to the sea, or the pleasures of a lonely beach in Northumberland. It meant a resort, a town by the sea, with bright lights and piers and pleasure beaches. Mostly it meant Bridlington or Scarborough or, on the Lancashire coast, Blackpool or Morecambe. Very occasionally, distant exotic places like Rhyl or Llandudno were mentioned and, where the father worked for the railways, the family enjoyed the privilege of free travel by train and could thus penetrate to places well beyond the reach of others – to Torquay and Bournemouth!

The most popular week of the year for these holidays was the first in August – Bank Holiday Week, for it was then that most mills and factories closed down entirely and Leeds had its Wakes Week. A few, mainly older, parents went away in September after the seasonal illuminations had begun in Blackpool and Morecambe, a piece of municipal enterprise intended to extend the attractions of the holiday season in a blaze of electric light bulbs.

Those unable to afford a holiday away from home could, in compensation, take a day excursion, either by train or charabanc to any of the resorts mentioned. Coach firms ran day trips from City Square or the Corn Exchange. There was usually no need to book in advance. A chalked blackboard showed the destination, time and price, if not of a seaside resort, then a trip round the Dales or to the Peak District, or to the ruined abbeys of the county. Greatly daring, there were trips in the evening, billed as Mystery Tours, route undisclosed, but quite likely to end up at "Dick Hudson's" on the Ilkley Moors.

Should these be out of reach, Leeds itself offered attractions which were available for only the modest tram fare. Roundhay Park was the most popular day out, but also within the city boundary were Kirkstall Abbey and the mansion at Temple Newsam for the historically inclined. More strenuous was to take the tram which wound along the side of the Aire Valley to Guiseley. From here it was a good climb on to the moor-top of Otley Chevin with great expanses of Wharfedale and the Washburn valley below. Or further west one could penetrate into the deep heather moors above Ilkley. At the end of the day it was obligatory to end up with fish and chips from

Harry Ramsden's shop before queueing for the tram back to Leeds.

Just outside the Leeds boundary was a private venture of the 1930s called Golden Acre Park. Economising, one took a tram to the Lawnswood terminus and walked along the main Otley Road – a long sweaty walk on a summer day, laden with a picnic bag and a cautious raincoat. Because it was a private enterprise there was an entrance fee, but inside there was a lake with a water-chute, a small smelly menagerie and a café infested by wasps. It never had the air of being a successful venture, failing to fulfil the expectations roused by the superlatives in which it was advertised in the local paper. If the weather was good, however, it was sufficently far into the country rather than being suburban, to enable one to display a sun-tanned face.

Given that Leeds people favoured a limited number of resorts and that they went there during the first week in August, the foundations existed for the seaside holiday to be very similar to being at home. Financial constraints meant staying in a boarding-house, mainly located in the back streets – the superior ones on the front charged extra. One therefore exchanged one street for another. It was often a street in which there were not even small gardens and was not in smelling distance of the sea, even though the houses carried names like 'Seaview' or 'Wave Crest' or 'Golden Sands'.

The boarding-houses themselves were, on the whole, grim establishments, usually old fashioned terrace houses. The proprietors lived somewhere below the ground floor. They ate, slept and cooked there, leading a troglodyt existence during the summer so that the house could hold as many visitors as possible. The only rooms above cellar level which were not bedrooms were the dining room, bathroom and W.C. The walls were thick with house-rules and prohibitions. No pets. No hot baths without an extra charge. No smoking in the bedrooms. No noise after 10 p.m. Breakfast, 8 o'clock prompt, dinner 12.30, supper (or sometimes High Tea) 6 p.m. Do not hang wet costumes out of the window. Leave buckets and spades outside. Please leave the W.C. as you would expect to find it. Bedrooms must be vacated by 10.30 a.m. on day of departure. Front door key available on request only. Switch off the landing light.

Boarding meant supplying one's own food which was cooked by the landlady and sometimes delivered to the dining room by dumb-waiter, to which one was summoned by hearing the number of one's table called from hidden depths. In the dining room there was a cupboard in which for each table there was a numbered shelf. The use of the cruet was charged as an extra item on the bill. Because the house, when fully booked, was overcrowded, so, therefore, was the dining room. It made for an atmosphere of bonhomie after the shyness of the first day, with the weather always available as the solvent which was guaranteed to loosen stiff tongues. Anyway, it was impossible to sit so tightly packed and remain isolated and aloof. Such close proximity of dining tables meant that it was all very intimate and there was plenty of scope for the exercise of that competitive spirit between neighbours which was such a powerful dynamic. It was expressed through food. What were No. 3 having today? Not fish again! Well, of course, it is nice and we are at the seaside, so it's ever so fresh and cheap too! But give me a piece of steak any day. Personally, I never did care for margarine on my bread. I've always insisted on paying extra for best butter. Yes, well, of course, Father never will go out on a morning until I've made him a hot breakfast, but, of course, a lot of people can't be bothered and are happy with a bowl of cornflakes. My word, Mr Horncastle, that looks a tasty little chop. Fancy you preferring sausages to a bit of good old English roast beef, Mrs Prothero. Still it'd be a dull world if we all liked the same things, wouldn't it?

And if not food, then the dresses of the ladies, a different one each day. Hot, covert glances, hastily converted into bright good-morning smiles as the latest contender in the fashion stakes entered the dining room. The men engaged in no similar contest. They wore much the same clothes each day, an item more or less depending on the weather. A tweed sports jacket and a pair of flannel trousers, perhaps a pullover. Shirts worn open at the neck. Old men often continued to wear heavy woollen underwear with the vest buttoned up to the neck, protruding above the shirt opening.

All out, as if by magic after meals. There was no sitting-room, and, if the rain poured daily, guests were not welcome in the house between meals, or in the evenings before bedtime. Bad weather was, therefore, an economic disaster, since families were forced to seek some sort of shelter which, at the seaside, meant paying money to be entertained. It was good news for the various freak shows and so-called entertainment arcades, which gobbled money – bad news for parents, faced with rapidly dwindling reserves and keeping the peace between fractious children.

The bedrooms did not have wash-basins installed. Instead, there were wash-stands, each with a ewer of cold water, a big bowl to pour it in, and an enamel slop bucket. There was usually a matching chamber pot in the small cupboard by the side of the bed. As a luxury for shavers, a can of hot water with a lid and spout was delivered outside the bedroom door when the landlady knocked on it early in the morning. There was, of course, only one bathroom. The bath was usually supplied with hot water by a malevolent-looking gas geyser. It was charged as an extra. There was also only one W.C. so that most people on holiday suffered a far worse ratio of persons per W.C. than at home, even if they lived in a fairly old back-to-back house. No sooner was one installed, having hovered nonchalantly in the offing, awaiting the departure of the previous occupant, or more modestly having lurked behind the bedroom door, one eye to its slightly open crack, than there would be a rattle of ill-concealed impatience on the handle. The pressure to vacate the establishment during the day meant that all the guests were looking for the same relief at about the same time – just after breakfast being most popular. Sometimes, in sheer desperation, it seemed that the public conveniences on the seafront might offer refuge. The problem was that sufferers from similarly congested boarding houses all over the town had already converged with only one thought in mind. It was, therefore, better to remain at one's post and to brazen it out, abandoning all pretence at modesty by taking up a firm stance on the landing, in defiance of all comers and then feigning deafness to any door-rattling. The bolt which fastened the door worked a rachet making the sign "Engaged" – and that, by God, was the truth!

The other guests in the house were, with different names and faces, the same people who lived in the street at home. Mainly they came from Leeds, if one went to the Yorkshire coast. Morecambe, on the west coast, was favoured by Bradford people, and Blackpool drew widely on the whole north. In both Lancashire resorts there would be people from mysterious places like Bury, Accrington, Salford and Rochdale – depending on the timing of their Wakes Weeks.

Added together, the town, the street, the house, the guests, all seemed to conspire to make a holiday by the sea dangerously like staying at home. But miraculously it wasn't! Not at all! The resorts themselves had, however unlikely it might seem, a magic quality, combining the presence of the sea, the sands, piers and funfairs and the novelty of it all. Above all, it was the atmosphere which, for the holiday-maker, was, after all, a do-it-yourself creation to a great extent. There was a sense of relaxation qualified only by a determination to enjoy it all. Extra money in one's pocket, the outcome of weeks of heroic abstinence, with gifts of 'holiday money' from parents and relatives, gave for the time being a wonderful sense of affluence. There were so many things to choose between.

People were avid for novelty and new sensations called for gratification. The first and most obvious were the sea and the beach and these accordingly were crowded on a fine day in the height of the season, especially towards the centre of the town. Indeed, as the tide came in, pushing the deckchairs closer and closer towards the sea-wall, the beach would become so packed that it resembled a busy shopping thoroughfare in Leeds town centre on a Saturday afternoon, even though further along the promenade in both directions there was plenty of space. Even in the sea itself there would be so many people splashing about that it was actually difficult to swim without leaving them behind and swimming well out to sea, provided, of course, that it was not too cold. This was more of a problem on the East Coast, lapped by the chilly waters of the North Sea. Those who had committed themselves bobbed up and down, quickly regretting their hardiness as they felt their feet and legs beginning to ache with cold. Screaming – as well they might – they splashed others, to show what good fun, how enjoyable it was. "Come on in!" they quavered invitingly. "The water's lovely!" What insincerity! Beyond them, the true swimmers battled gamely. The breast stroke was the most popular style, but, here and there, some product of swimming lessons at the swimming baths back home cut impressively through the water with a version of the 'crawl'. Closer to the edge where the sea ran in smooth sheets, shallow on the sand, older people paddled. The men had their trousers rolled up around the calves of their legs; the women had tucked their skirts into the elastic of their bloomers. Old feet, corns and bunions, old legs, white fleshed with blue and varicose veins outstanding, trudged through the sea's margin. It was generally believed that paddling in the sea was good for you.

In the zealous pursuit of a good time there was always a 'Pleasure Beach' available, the most famous being at Blackpool. Here, the joys which lasted only for two or three days at the nearest local 'Feast' were permanently on offer. There were, however, added attractions, particularly the gut-wrenching, heart-pounding, terrifying rides on the roller coasters. Again, the most notorious of these was at Blackpool. On the 'Big Dipper' screaming was obligatory, as the rattling cars plunged alarmingly down precipitous tracks and hurtled round bends which were so acute that it seemed certain that they must fly off at a tangent. Once committed there was no getting off. Many simply held tight with their eyes shut tight until they were released. Screaming featured on other rides. It was muffled to the outside world on the 'Ghost Train' as, in the blackness, mechanical hands grabbed and the ropes of simulated spiders' webs trailed unexpectedly across cringing faces, and suddenly illuminated skeletons passed so near that they could have touched the passenger. The quality of the screaming was different on the 'Cake Walk' and on the trip round Noah's Ark, when, at intervals, sudden upward thrusting jets of compressed air sent skirts flying up, revealing gratifying expanses of thighs and knickers which were a staple of seaside humour, from the pier-end comic to the greetings card.

For this week of the year the holiday-makers drew not only upon their savings of cash, but upon funds of repressed folly which, for the remaining 51 weeks, had lain fallow. One expression of this was to send comic risqué postcards to unsuitable recipients. Bums, bosoms, water closets, knickers, excretion, wind, great fat domineering ladies sitting astride tiny donkeys or perching on the laps of small henpecked husbands, scantily clad, anatomically grotesque young women suggesting all manner of things to improbable young men were stock figures of this fantasy world. They were Rabelaisian characters designed to bring the frostiest of sniffs from the person on whose doormat they landed. Saucy postcards showed that the sender was a proper 'card', not to mention a 'caution' or a 'one and full of it' – all different ways of referring to the same prized quality. Another sign of this was the wearing of comic hats bearing jokey messages to advertise the shedding of inhibitions by the wearer. The most popular was probably "Kiss Me Quick!" "Hello Sailor!" was a popular greeting and the influence of Mae West was evident in countless invitations to "Come Up And See Me Some Time". In any one year there would very likely be a 'craze'. In one year it might be for wooden bats with rubber balls attached by a piece of elastic – very hazardous for unwary passers-by on a crowded promenade. In the following year it was the 'Yo-Yo', or perhaps the 'bazooka' or 'Tommy Talker', tin mouth instruments which, when played, emitted a raucous noise. The possession of one of these was *de rigeur* – not to have one was to suffer bitter envy and a sharp down-grading in caste.

The fashions in pleasure-seeking were otherwise less ephemeral. Fathers, whose usual response to a new day was surly and bad tempered, arose early and went for a jaunty stroll along the promenade before breakfast, breathing deeply to obtain maximum benefit from the ozone, which was reputed to be good for you, though in reality it was a compound smell of rotting seaweed, dead fish and, not infrequently, sewage which was poured into the sea. Sunday morning, apart from a look at the *News of the World*, still had Sabbatarian constraints, indissoluble even in the relaxed climate of the seaside. It was the occasion for a sedate stroll, dressed in one's best clothes, along the promenade. In Morecambe, for example, the most favoured route was to the neighbouring village of Heysham. Here, custom dictated that the stroller should drink a glass of nettle beer. Necessity rather than custom then required a visit to a privately owned lavatory for which one penny was charged by the custodian who, having sold the nettle beer, made a double profit. Then back along the promenade at a rather more purposeful pace, to arrive in time for the Sunday dinner which had been cooking below stairs – the cabbage foully done to death and served in a bilious shade of poisonous green which it owed to a good helping of bicarbonate of soda.

Whatever the fashions, they had in common not only the pursuit of health and enjoyment but, at least as important, the acquisition of proof that the pursuit had been successful. The most obvious evidence was, of course, a tan, whatever the agonies in getting it. With only a week's holiday on the one hand and the uncertainty of the weather on the other, this meant the maximum exposure of flesh permissible for as long as possible. There was insufficient time to heed the warnings of medical men about the dangers of sunburn and the wisdom of increasing gradually the length of exposure to the sun. Uneasy nights, sore arms, blistered backs and faces, were not only to be endured. They were badges of rank.

In addition to arriving back home with as brown a face as possible, it was also important to have put weight on as further proof that the holiday had done you good. It was, therefore, obligatory to be weighed on the first day of the holiday and again on the last. Some weighing machines were automatic, either with a dial and pointer or with a mechanism which coughed out a piece of card on which one's weight was inscribed together, with an encouraging piece of prophecy: "Good Luck Will Come Your way!" or "This Could Be Your Year For Romance!". None of these machines, no matter how pointed or optimistic were their forecasts, compared in popularity with the man who tended the great polished brass scales in which the customer sat in a plush-bottomed seat suspended from a sort of tripod and was balanced against proper weights. It was situated on the promenade. The ceremony, into which the simple act of getting weighed had been converted, was, therefore, made public and an occasion of fun. There seemed to be an endless supply of fat, jolly ladies. Even the fattest of customers were pleased to have increased their weight by a few pounds, for how otherwise could good have been done?

Not least of the treats to be enjoyed during the week was a visit one evening to the resident concert party on the Pier, or in the Winter Gardens – the "Follies" or "Fol-de-Rols" or simply "Pierrots". There was always a comedian, hired for the whole season, who told dialect stories in a Yorkshire or Lancashire accent and always knew which towns were having their Wakes Week, slipping into his patter jokes relating specially to them. Another prop who helped to carry the show was always a baritone who sang, first, rousing and jolly songs, and finished with powerfully philosophical and reflective songs, like one called *Leaning*, inducing in the audience a quiet, almost pensive mood of the 'You Could Have Heard A Pin Drop' kind, before the comedian erupted back on stage with his seemingly inexhaustible supply of jokes about bums and bloomers. The show always began with the whole troupe, usually dressed in pierrot and columbine costumes, greeting the audience with a cheery song with words like:

> "Hello everybody! How do you do?
> We're here to entertain you
> And stop you feeling blue (etc., etc.) "

There surely could never have been audiences more predisposed to being entertained. What did it matter if the landlady was a bit of a dragon, if there was always sand on the bedroom floor? Who cared about lumpy beds and the fact that it was already Wednesday and the stored-up magic was already half exhausted and the holiday sliding quickly downhill to Saturday, when there would be a sharp end to the meagre hospitality of one's boarding-house? Thoughts like these were dispelled by the pleasure of the moment. Why brood over the inevitable? But whose pot of jam, whose jar of pickled onions, whose tinned beans and boiled ham would usurp one's shelf in the dining room cupboard? No miraculous intervention would postpone the dawning of Saturday morning and the dismal luggage-encumbered trudge to the station, burdened additionally now with the small paraphernalia of a seaside holiday: a tin spade, bent in the middle of the blade, its red paint worn away and rust already showing; a bucket with some seawater and minor marine creatures in it, far advanced along the road to death.

On the train all those who had been so cheery on the way to the coast would be muted and some children would weep as the train pulled slowly out of the station which, unlike that at home, was bright with hanging baskets of flowers. Not only the journey home, but at least a whole year stretched ahead. It was unthinkable!

The human spirit is remarkably resilient, however. On one's return, the house looked different – the dimensions of the rooms seemed to have changed and each one had to be inspected. And there were friends to impress with stories of the holidays, though their unfamiliarity with the circumstances reduced their interest so one didn't bother. Provided that one were back in time and that there was sixpence left or, more likely, that parents could be induced to extend a token of last week's bounty, there would surely be something 'on' at one of the local cinemas. A quick injection of Disney, or Laurel and Hardy, who frequently featured as 'B' movies, and the process of recovery would be complete. If the woman in the box office overlooked one's age, there might even be a good murder showing.

CHAPTER 9

Sundays and Sex

Sunday. In the middle of the nineteenth century authority had conducted a huge statistical enquiry, concerned at the apparent lack of religious observance amongst the working classes [the religious census of 1851]. The results generally confirmed the worst fears. An urban proletariat was revealed which was apparently Godless – if such a condition could be measured by counting the numbers attending places of worship. Had anyone bothered to conduct a similar investigation in the 1930s, the people in our street would surely have yielded a similar impression. There were one or two households from which, dressed in their Sunday-best clothes and carrying some religious book like a talisman, there issued at least once on Sunday – sometimes twice – families displaying their piety in the faces of the indifferent and ungodly. They were chapel-goers bound for the ugly red brick tabernacle which stood next door to the Workhouse at the bottom of the hill. In one case they were going to take the tram to the more distant suburbs from which they had originated and whose chapel had continued to command their loyalty. The women of this family had a formidable reputation as singers. They were tiny, aggressive women with voices of such disproportionate power to their size as to swamp the rest of the congregation's more modest efforts. This was reported back when, as neighbours, they attended one of the weddings or funerals which took place from our street.

Otherwise, no one in the street bothered about church-going on Sunday except the single family who were somehow suspect, alien and apart, because they were Catholics! The parents attended a different church and socialised in a different club. Their numerous children went to different schools. They seemed less consciously virtuous and stiff than the chapel-goers when they all trooped off to Mass and much more relaxed and happy when they returned. A few streets away there was family of Salvationists, who actually rejoiced on Sunday when they put on their uniforms. The women carried tambourines with streamers attached to them and the men trombones, euphoniums, cornets and the like. Not only did they go to church, they brought their church to us, touring the streets with their bands and choirs. With brisk and cheerful efficiency they collected from door to door, as their songs of praise reverberated between rows of houses. They never actually 'saved' anyone in our street but they certainly cheered things up.

66

Vestigial traces of the gloomier aspects of religion were evident in our household, especially on Sundays. The feelings of discomfort activated by a stiff pre-breakfast dose of whatever laxative was currently in favour were intensified and prolonged by all sorts of prohibitions, seemingly aimed at making the day miserable. Oddly enough, attendance at Sunday School was never made compulsory, after an initial and unsuccessful introduction to organised religion. Nevertheless, there was a general blight on Sundays, partly to do with it being ordained as a day of rest, which in practice meant being seen but not heard. No games were allowed, either indoor or outdoor. Playing with toys was equally forbidden, the most that was allowed being to read the *Children's Encyclopedia*. The ban on games was made more irksome and reinforced by having to wear one's best clothes. A walk was permitted. This aching boredom was commonly the experience of friends who were from the same suburb and niche in the social hierarchy. Subdued, we met in the afternoon and went for walks, taking care not to do anything of a rough and tumble nature which would be sure to imperil those stiff and uncomfortable outfits.

The strict observance of the Sabbath was the most obvious way in which religion impinged. It did not exercise other than an oblique influence detectable, if at all, by the exercise of hindsight, when it came to relations between the sexes. For me, and as far as I can judge, for my immediate circle of acquaintances, these were characterised by ignorance and innocence, however reluctantly maintained on our part. There was no sex education at the elementary school before the age of eleven, or at the Grammar School for the rest of one's transition into adulthood. A single sex school, the only females with whom one came into contact were the Headmaster's Secretary who took on something of her Olympian employer's awesome divinity and was hardly to be thought of as a human being, and two formidable moustached ladies in the Junior School with whom one had no direct dealings and only saw in the corridor. Biology lessons were the nearest approach to unravelling the Great Mystery. Even though we dissected rabbits and drew diagrams in differently coloured pencils, it remained knowledge about rabbits. Furthermore, although one had in consequence a rough idea of the particular parts of rabbits, I do not recall that any explanation was given when – or indeed how – they were brought into relation with each other. It was all very abstract, but I can't remember being at all frustrated by the failure to make clear the mating habits of rabbits and their relevance to human beings.

Sexual knowledge of a kind, warped, furtively acquired and mostly a grotesque caricature of the truth, was bandied about by groups of boys in out-of-the way places, but it was not, even at this level, sought by the generality of boys and, therefore, remained as the not very valuable property of comparatively few. My friends and acquaintances who went on scholarships to the local high school had the advantage of attending a co-educational school in which they were in closer contact with girls. But although they were more prone to snigger knowingly and whisper among themselves and guffaw at some tit-bit, they failed to communicate the secrets which they shared, and I suspect that they were not much further ahead than we were in our monastic establishment.

The level of satisfying misinformation at which we operated is illustrated by a conversation which I held with a friend. He confided in me that he had worked out the mystery of where babies come from. As he had two younger sisters this seemed to qualify him as an authority. He had, he said, observed a scar on his mother's neck, the evidence of some previous operation, I later realised. That, he was sure, was the route by which babies arrived. The breathtaking implausibility of this theory was no barrier to its immediate acceptance. It seemed an entirely satisfying explanation of a matter which after all, had not exercised us very much in the first place and was not much more improbable than the truth. Having had one of the mysteries of human biology thus cleared up, further enlightenment was not long deferred.

One summer evening, after tea, my mother went for a walk – without father. This was unprecedented: what could it portend? Father broke what seemed to be a very long silence. He had been meaning to have a talk with me. Another long silence followed while he searched for suitable words. There were girls, he said, and there were boys and they were different from each other. I agreed that this was so and waited encouragingly for more pointed revelations. "You never had a sister," he said. Where was this conversation leading? It turned out that I was to behave with girls as though they had been this insubstantial sister. On subsequent reflection in later and better informed life, this seemed to be a pretty constraining counsel, unless one accepted implications which would have horrified my poor parent. And that was it – the sum total of knowledge to equip a boy for life. Except that, shortly afterwards, my parents purchased a thick black-bound volume from a door-to-door salesman. It bore the title *Vitalogy*[1] in gold letters and it was very thick. It was published in America. It was left casually, where I could not fail to see it, open at the page headed "Self-Pollution". Everything nasty, all manner of horrible diseases, would result from engaging in this 'secret vice', branding the sinner in the eyes of the world, and culminating in raging insanity. It seemed, furthermore, that there was this young man – I think he was called Burton, from Harrisburg Pa. – who had fallen victim to this degrading vice. He was pictured 'before' and, overleaf, 'after'. The crude way in which lines had been drawn on his face to indicate gross dissipation did not deter me from identifying a kindred spirit. Admittedly the accompanying diatribe did not spell out precisely what Mr.Harris had done with such dramatic consequences, but an already guilty conscience identified the almost certain cause. It was TOO LATE! For a long time I suffered agonies of shame and remorse as I waited for the consequences to manifest themselves. Every spot was seen as the onset of terminal disease, or the harbinger of the van in which I would be taken away in a strait-jacket. This was in the middle of the 1930s, not Victorian England, when such literature circulated freely and, I imagine, with as little success among its terror-stricken readers in ending a harmless practice. It can hardly be said that school, parents, or friends imparted other than the most arrant nonsense,

---

[1]Ruddock, E. H. *Vitalogy: An Encyclopedia of Health and Home* (Vitalogy Association, Chicago, 1930), first published in 1896 and going through many editions, the 1930 one being probably the last.

at worst, or embarrassed platitudes at best. How easily one accepted these gross caricatures of reality, when a little reflection and the use of commonsense would have exposed them as the rubbish they were. I do not know how widely such dross currency circulated. I do not know how far my ignorance of sex in its totality was shared by others.

At about this time, an episode happened to me which illustrated the depths of my ignorance. As a future pupil at the Grammar School I pre-empted the situation by going into the Park wearing the conspicuous cap to which my scholarship entitled me, feeling very superior. What happened as a result was probably well deserved. I came up to about half a dozen girls who were all bigger than me. As I made to go past them, one snatched my cap off my head, the whole pack running toward some thick bushes. I ran after them, concerned about the fate of my cap, into the bushes, where they turned on me. I was no match for six bigger girls. I was soon spreadeagled under them, looking up at the trees. Not for long. One pulled up her skirts and sat on my face. The others followed in due course. They were all wearing navy blue knickers as was the custom of the time for schoolgirls. They were probably girls from one of the senior classes at school who inhabited the unknown part, which was forbidden territory. Anyway, I did not recognise them, not that I had much opportunity, as one followed another in quick succession, scarcely giving me time to draw breath, let alone recognise my captors and tormentors. The nature of the assault was unknown to me, that it had anything to do with sex would have come as a complete shock. I remained as ignorant as before and, truth to tell, did not find the experience of being sat on disagreeable, once I found that I could breathe (with difficulty), that mostly their weight was tolerable and the smell of their knickers strangely exciting. Why this was so I hadn't the faintest idea. Presumably they had. I should remember them more clearly – not what they looked like, but their conversation – for example, what did they talk about while I was at their mercy, were they concerned in any way about my ability to breathe under them – I might have suffocated. Was their pleasure when astride my face so great that they were incapable of speech? I never knowingly saw one of them again, never encountered them as a victim, or any similar behaviour by girls. The whole episode remained a mystery to me. Memory provided no clue.

My failure to understand what was happening to me was a state of mind, I am sure, which was encouraged, if not explained, by the enormous popularity of the cinema and its slurring-over of reality. One sat entranced, watching the antics of people – with all the authority conveyed by the 'star' system – who never went to bed with each other. Although making love to each other, they never were shown in sexually explicit situations. Sex was, at most, hinted at in a titillating way and the screen abounded in erotic images which always faded in the face of the direction in which the couple were going and baulked at a conclusion except one which – using a different medium – authors indicated by dots, thus . . . It was a world of dots and innuendo. The kind of song sung by George Formby with his 'little stick of Blackpool rock' and 'Mr Wu and the window cleaner' were always good for a knowing snigger. Or Max Miller in love with Mary from the Dairy; or Mae West whom everybody, it seemed imitated, being sure of a tired laugh by repeating: "Come up and and see me some time". What would happen if one

69

did so? I don't think that any of us had the faintest idea. I would, I suppose, have tried to treat her like a sister!

There were girls in one's life who, on occasion, aroused blind, painful yearnings which could ruin appetite, but these did not translate themselves into sexual terms. The condition was known as 'Calf Love'. It was a subject of mild derision amongst adults, but it was acute and real and very distressing to adolescent boys. The opportunity to peform deeds of conspicuous daring and gallantry, culminating in fantasies of rescuing the object of desire from a variety of deadly perils never seemed to arise. There was a marked absence of burning buildings, runaway horses and deadly snakes, nothing to require the ice-cold courage and subsequent self-effacement – not too much, though, just sufficient to culminate in one of those last reel shots of the hero and heroine deeply embracing as the music swelled and the film ended – just in time to prevent any consummation. It would be enough . . . what more was there?

The innocence in which early adolescence was spent extended to the use of bad language. We didn't use it because we didn't know any. We were not being sheltered: it simply did not arise. On occasions when strong emotions were indicated the speaker in a book or article in a magazine was allowed to use asterisks. Much later than the time of which I am writing, people used expressions like 'mucking' and 'basket' in books or in the cinema. But the real-life words for which they were substitutes were not used in the time – the 1930s – and the place – the world of the respectable working class in south Leeds.

Nor was the dirty joke current. I remember hearing the lines:
"It wasn't the Almighty
Who lifted her nighty.
It was Roger, the lodger, the sod."
Indeed, although I cannot recall where I heard them, they so impressed me as being witty that I proudly recited them to my parents, expecting praise for the humour which they encapsulated. Without warning, the roof fell in. Deep disgrace was the result of this attempt to entertain. There was nothing between the stout covers of *Vitalogy* to explain what Roger intended, let alone why it was a taboo topic in polite circles.

CHAPTER 10

Health and Illness

Although, like sex, surrounded by misinformation and prejudice, health and illness were subjects of everyday life and discussion. The common affliction of constipation brought two kinds of remedy. Firstly there were the much advertised patent medicines, ranging from various kinds of salts – liver, Glauber, and what were euphemistically called Fruit Salts. There were proprietary laxatives cunningly trying to disguise their fundamental nastiness under a coating of mint-flavoured chocolate and, of course, the nauseous fluid Californian Syrup of Figs. Secondly, there were purgatives which were non-proprietary and represented in some cases the survival of folk medicine, but were without exception foul: cascara, senna pods, flowers of sulphur, powdered magnesia, liquorice powder, Epsom salts and a mixture of brimstone and treacle. A distinction should be made, between the ominously called 'opening medicines' used regularly – weekly, or in more stubborn cases, more frequently and those concoctions held in reserve, like regiments of crack troops, a *corps d'élite*, used for special duty. They appeared in the spring, roughly coincidental with the annual orgy of spring cleaning, which was the season when it was popularly held that specially potent medicines were needed to 'purify the blood'. Whole families were lined up to be dosed with brimstone and treacle which had been prepared in a stone jar. Whatever distinctions might be drawn between them, whether they were described as purgatives, laxatives, aperients, they had one thing in common, they were vile to take, and no conciliatory spoonfuls of jam or sweets could disguise this fact. The harm that they wrought is incalculable.

The regular dosing with what was alarmingly called 'opening medicine', giving rise to such phrases as, "Have you had your bowels opened?" could well elicit the reply, "No!", from the literal minded, leading to another dose of purgative, which was one recipe for good health. Otherwise there was cod liver oil in various forms. You could drink it neat, which was the heroic method, or for frailer spirits it came in a variety of disguises masking the fishy flavour. There was a pale yellow version called 'Angiers Emulsion', which was thick and tasted worse. Preferable were the various brands of combination with malt extract. Some of these were, to my mind, so nice that I made secret raids on the source of supply. The most popular alternative was Scott's Emulsion which depicted on its label a fisherman in sou'wester and boots with a giant cod slung over his shoulder. I liked this and could never understand the caprice which made my mother opt for one of the others.

The common cold was the thing which, in winter, was perpetual and against which there was no defence. There were no paper tissues available and the prevailing forms of toilet paper which could act as a substitute, where the household had progressed beyond newspaper, was scratchy and abrasive. Milled to present an unyielding shiny surface, or unmilled but equally uncongenial to one's tenderer parts, they had clearly been designed by a sadist and were totally unsuited for nasal application. Not only did they make it sore, but, not being absorbent, it was difficult to ensure that the snot did not glissade off the paper, ending up in some embarrassing place. The tissue paper that baker's bread was wrapped in was passable but, by its nature, likely to be scarce.

Handkerchiefs were heavily used and were always part of the bounty of Christmas and birthdays. The best were large Irish linen, soft and soothing, or made from Sea Island cotton. But they were rare because they were expensive. Donors preferred quantity to quality, so one had to be grateful for nose-wipes more suited to one's station. Cheaper cotton handkerchiefs were therefore commonly in use. There were also coarse larger versions, suitable for workmen, in colours like khaki, or red spotted ones in which, traditionally, the lunch time 'snap' was carried. For people of little account, like children, mothers often cut up cotton flour bags, or dismembered sheets which had been patched or turned beyond repair. Young children were sent to school with one of these increasingly unsavoury objects pinned to the jersey, if a boy, dress or pinafore, if girls – who also had a pocket in the leg of their navy blue knickers, or stuffed the handkerchief past the elastic of the knicker leg. Whatever form the handkerchief took, it was to be carried, otherwise, in a pocket, growing more and more soggy as the day progressed. Discarded by its owner to form part of the weekly wash, it was added to the collection of unspeakable germ-laden slimy objects to be laundered. No one seemed to question the necessity for one's mother to clean this disgusting haul.

Once contracted, there was little one could do except wait for the cold to get better of its own accord, or worse – like turning into 'flu, bronchitis or pneumonia. There were proprietary substances which were designed to alleviate the misery of a blocked-up nose. One sprinkled a few drops on a handkerchief and breathed deeply of the vapours released, if it were possible to breathe through one's nose at all! Other products like 'Vick' Brand 'Vapour Rub' were smeared on the chest and around the nostrils at bedtime to release their mentholated balm in bed. Different people had sure remedies by which they swore. A whole onion boiled in milk – though some said eaten raw – was one. Others placed their faith in hot toddies of various substances combined with whisky or rum and consumed on going to bed. If the cold turned into a sore throat, one of the most bizarre alleged cures was to go to bed with a dirty sock wound round the throat. If the cold turned into 'flu, as most high temperatures were called, the object was to make the sufferer sweat profusely by various means. There was the ordeal of the mustard bath, usually combined with the application of hot water bottles. These and the heaping of plenty of bedclothes on top of the victim ensured copious sweating and acute discomfort for hours. There were also proprietary and other medicines. Fennings Fever Cure was a remedy always to hand. It was bitter enough to make you contort your face. Or you could ask the local chemist to make up a non-proprietary mixture containing, I think, paregoric and saltpeter amongst other ingredients. If the treatment worked one emerged in the morning feeling weak and looking pale, speaking in what was known as a 'pale blue' voice, to be very likely fed either on 'pobs' – pieces of bread soaked in hot milk and sugar – or perhaps an egg whisked in milk. Later in the day there would probably be beef tea, and, if all went well, one would be let out of bed to sit by the fireside, wrapped in a blanket.

If all did not go well and the 'flu was obstinate, the Doctor would be sent for. In the days before antibiotics there was little he could do other than prescribe bed and rest and keep a look out for complications or the development of other more sinister symptoms. However, he dignified one's condition, setting it on to an altogether higher plane by arriving at the house in a motor-car which was in itself an indication that something was seriously wrong. No longer did he rely, as was once said in *The Lancet*, on a paunch for dignity, a top hat for authority and piles for an anxious expression, as had his Victorian predecessor. A Wolsey Hornet may have lacked the charismatic qualities of his forerunner's horse-drawn equipage, with a groom to drive it, but the arrival of anyone in a car in our street was rare enough to be dramatic. In the absence of a National Health Service and not being members of any other scheme, the visit would have to be paid for out of our own pockets. The summoning of the doctor was, therefore, a measure of the seriousness of the case and one could be sure that as soon as his car had gone there would be visits from the neighbours and the word would spread in the sort of official language which the doctor had used, to be subjected to minute inspection and speculation, with some added exaggeration.

It might be the case that the illness was not 'flu but the onset of something more serious. In fact, the memory of the great and highly lethal influenza epidemic which followed the war was still vivid, particularly for my mother who had caught it. A suspected case was, therefore, not treated lightly. The status of 'flu was therefore very high, higher than some of the diseases which commonly swept through the child population and which lacked the more serious implications which have since been attributed to them. These left the child in no more than a fractious state, away from school and getting under its mother's feet in a small house. Mumps, measles, chicken-pox and German measles were thus disparaged as being excessively disruptive, though measles was recognised as having possible serious complications. Beyond these there lurked other sinister diseases which always seemed to be present and sometimes flared into epidemics.

The commonest of these were diphtheria and scarlet fever. There were also, from time to time, outbreaks of infantile paralysis. Diphtheria and scarlet fever required the patient to be isolated in a fever hospital, though scarlet fever might possibly be treated at home as it had been earlier in the century. This involved draping the sickroom door with sheeting to prevent the spread of infection to other members of the family. Otherwise, one was taken to Killingbeck Hospital, part of which acted as a sanatorium for the treatment of tubercular patients. The patient was given a number and bulletins were printed in the evening paper, divided into categories: Very Poorly, Rather Poorly, Friends May Visit, etc., followed by the patients' numbers. I always spent a melancholy few minutes scanning this item, even though I knew no one who was an inmate. There were awful stories of what might happen to you in hospital and reading the list of numbers gave a vicarious thrill. Sometimes one followed the fortunes of a particular patient hiding behind a number. Most progressed up the scale of categories, but some declined and, in the harrowing death bed scenes enacted in the imagination, it was oneself occupying the central but transient role.

T.B., or consumption as it was known popularly, might, almost certainly would, involve a protracted stay in the sanatorium, which had open verandahs along its length, partitioned for occupation by the patients, for whom fresh air, rest and sunshine were key factors in the fight against the disease. They were visible from the tram on the express track, by the side of the main road to York. It was a disease with high mortality which so often overtook characters in Victorian literature and it was probably the shadows of this often melodramatic image which still dominated popular notions of the disease, which, after all, was still a very real threat. There were fearful references to it in voices suitably lowered. Rumour had it that the patients were kept out in the fresh air, even to having snow on their beds – always at least a foot of snow. A thin neck, at the back, was thought to be a sure sign of the imminence of the disease. Most awe-inspring of all was 'galloping consumption', in which the patient was presumably in reduced health, so that the disease swept through the patient 'like wildfire' and, after the passage of a few weeks, ended in his demise. Long faces and hushed tones were obligatory in reference to the disease to which some degree of social stigma attached because of its relation to poverty. It was furthermore contagious and therefore the victim was a potential danger to others.

Of the other contagious diseases which were a menace to public health, syphilis and gonorrhoea, were the subject of a crashing silence. One was kept in total ignorance of them even though they must have featured prominently in the public mind. There had recently been the First World War, with its high rate of male participation as members of the Forces and a much increased incidence of venereal disease as a consequence of the war itself, but this was not reflected by public discussion in society. There were, in some public toilets, enamel plates advising the person to whom such a message was relevant to visit a hospital where they were promised complete confidence, but the language in which such messages were conveyed was oblique and only meaningful to an inner core of men who had reason to suspect that they might have been at risk. Once again *Vitalogy* was no help at all, with its evasive language and euphemisms.

Resort was had to a doctor only when it seemed that the patient was seriously ill, having resisted the exposure to treatment by patent medicine or remedies of greater antiquity, derived often from an otherwise forgotten rural past as folk medicine. In addition to the remedies for colds, there were others. Pennyroyal was for ill-defined 'women's complaints' for which Indian Brandee was also recommended. Like a number of medicines it was sold at the corner shop, displayed on stiff white cardboard to which the bottles were fixed by elastic bands. They were most usually manufactured by Parkinson's of Burnley, or Beecham's of St. Helens. Laxatives were probably the most prolific of these medicines, reflecting the place which constipation occupied in working-class life as a suspected source of ill-health. They were closely rivalled by aids to digestion. Both were popular as antidotes to working-class diet, which was heavy in cheap bulk foods. Bread and potatoes, pikelets, muffins and ovencakes fresh from the baker's shop, smeared with beef or pork dripping were, I am sure, productive of both constipation and chronic indigestion together. Dumplings and Yorkshire puddings did not help.

The incomes earned by the sort of people of whom I am writing were by no means lavish. Five pounds a week was spoken of as a kind of bench-mark which only few attained and which was the object of envy. For those in regular work, however, things were not so tightly ordered as to make such a diet dominated by carbohydrate foods absolutely necessary. They had been the traditional belly-fillers of previous generations of working-class consumers, for whom the first consideration had been the filling of hungry families. It was one's grandmothers, reared in this tradition who had imparted their culinary knowledge, or lack of it, to our mothers who were still serving a dietary which belonged to yesteryear, rather than reflecting the possibilities open to them. Poor diet was admittedly a much worse problem for the health of those in the lower echelons of the working class, or those who were unemployed. Rickets, for example, was still a problem, though by no means as severe as it had been for older generations. It was mainly among the parental generation stretching back to the 1890s and older people that there was evidence of bone malformation. The two ladies opposite, whose choral contributions were so vivid, were not only very short, suggesting dietary deficiency in their earlier years, but had quite striking bow legs. They were the only ones in our street, but their affliction, or 'K legs', which bent inwards rather than outwards were common. They were a subject for ribaldry, not sympathy – "Couldn't stop a pig in a ginnel", was one way of referring to the problem. Another, sung at the tops of our voices, without any recognition of its true meaning, but nonetheless cruel was the jingle:

"Ting-a-ling, crash, bang!
Get a woman, if you can,
If you can't get a woman
Get a bow legged man!"

In our time, children thought by school medical officers to be in danger of developing the disease were sent for sun-lamp treatment. There was also available cheap or free milk in needy cases, which was distributed in school during morning classes and sucked through straws inserted in a hole which could be pressed in the centre of the cardboard bottle top. The rude noises which could be made by sucking in air as the milk approached the bottom of the bottle came as a brilliant novelty to each sucessive generation of children. They really were straws!

Measures such as these were a twentieth-century answer to a nineteenth-century problem. Otherwise, I think that in many ways our lives were still dominated by the values and customs of the previous century. One illustration of the time-lag by which the received popular wisdom of the previous century, long since discredited, was the 'miasmic theory' of the spread of disease. This was the notion that diseases such as cholera were spread by the inhaling of foul smells which resulted from the accumulations of filth all too common in nineteenth-century towns and cities. In summer when the weather was hot, the drains by the sides of the pavement, not having their contents renewed with fresh rainwater, became stagnant and smelled. They were known significantly as 'fever grates'. When approaching the grates which were regularly placed in the kerbside gutters, we drew breath and held it until the objectionable source of the bad smell had been passed, repeating this stratagem for avoiding fever every time a grate came into view.

This made our progress along the pavement appear even more erratic than it was already, given the necessity of avoiding treading on the cracks between the stone flags in order to avert whatever disaster would otherwise result: a variable term of bad luck, or the death of one's mother (which would also happen if one picked hedge parsley, popularly known as 'mother-die'). If you crossed your fingers immunity was obtained. This was very necessary in the hot summer weather when the tar between the paving stones melted and produced shining bubbles which popped very satisfactorily when trodden on. If, of course, there were hop-scotch pitches drawn on the pavement, it was obligatory to launch into a series of hops, skips and jumps. Walking along the pavement was not simply a matter of getting from A to B, but a highly ritualised means of progression fraught with all kinds of awful consequences. It never crossed our minds that the majority of people appeared to ignore the rules which we observed and remain unaffected.

The Corporation tried to mitigate the effects of dry hot weather by sending round muck-carts to bear away the offensive accumulations in the grates and flush them with fresh water. It was a big, high-sided cart into which the foul matter was deposited with the use of a scoop, another of the horse-drawn vehicles inhabiting the street. The Corporation muck-carts were known, naturally, as 'fever-carts' and were the subject of a jingle which began, promisingly:

The Corporation muck cart was full up to the brim,
The Corporation driver fell in and couldn't swim,
He sank right to the bottom, just like a little stone . . .

It concluded:

More work for the undertaker
Another little job for the tombstone maker.

CHAPTER 11

Relations

With seven uncles on my mother's side of the family and three more on the other side, it is not surprising that uncles are more dominant in my memory than aunts. Of these, one was not really an aunt. It was not referred to, indeed I fail to recall any occasion on which her origins were mentioned, but there must have been one, or how did I know that she was not a real aunt? She occupied her place as the eldest daughter without comment and was simply Auntie Laura, wife of Uncle Frank Wilson, mother of Kathleen who was a leading light in the chapel, known as The Railway Mission on Eighteenth Avenue, of which my grandparents were the caretakers and which was responsible for a great deal of misery, which, along with unemployment, general poverty and bad housing, hung miasma-like over that part of Leeds. The devotees of this particular branch of Christianity held that it was sinful to go to the cinema or to any form of theatrical performance, and, incredibly to me, cousin Kathleen had been to neither, her leisure time being spent in praying for the souls of those who had.

Still, all this piety was not sufficient to save Uncle Frank from being found one Sunday afternoon in *flagrante delicto* on the sitting-room hearthrug with Auntie Gertie – the younger of the two remaining daughters of my paternal grandparents – who concealed a lusty appetite under a pious exterior. Of her, more in due course. Her sister, Auntie Annie, was also unwed, and remained so, her role being to stay at home and care for her father and mother in their old age, by which time her hopes of marriage had long ago been stifled, as both grandparents lived long lives. Annie would, by common consent, have made a good mother. No one thought there was any hypocrisy involved in saying this, or that care of the old couple could have been shared more equitably. Annie was just there and accepted her role without question.

The other member of the household was Uncle John who was deaf as a post. A powerfully built man, he had the misfortune to lose his hearing as a consequence of catching scarlet fever when a child. There were no deaf aids available under the National Health Scheme and John never had enough money to buy one privately. He drifted in and out of the fringes of the casual labour market, his deafness making it difficult for him to hold a job, particularly in the economically depressed 1930s. He was a willing worker, always ready with his shovel to clear the pavements of snow when extra men were needed for this task by the Corporation. Living in his own world, smiling at some inner source of pleasure, he worked in the backyard where he had cobbled together a sort of shed in which he could work. He made things from bits of scrap wood. Perhaps it was this which caused his artefacts to be unsatisfactory – lop-sided, or top heavy, too big or too small for the job for which they were intended. Working with raw materials which were the wrong size or shape to start with he was doomed to failure from the initial concept. Like the bogy he made to carry the weekly shopping from the Co-op. It was big enough to carry the entire stock of the shop and it was a practical failure. It lay under some sacking in the backyard, large and unwanted, rather like John in the labour market.

John's weakness was his throat. He never had a plain sore throat but was prone to 'quinsies', which were a mysterious affliction from which no one else with whom I was familiar seemed to suffer. The treatment was pretty dramatic involving the painting of the throat with a camel-hair brush soaked in iodine. John seemed to have attacks coinciding with gatherings of the family and would, for the most part, be a hidden presence upstairs in bed. Sometimes, however, he would simulate delirium, first putting on a warm dressing-gown and then lurching to the chair nearest the fire, where he would sit surveying the company through half-closed eyes and muttering incomprehensibly and, I suspect, critically, about each in turn. A thoroughly intimidating figure. But he was always persuaded back to his bed, usually by Auntie Annie, and stumped off with a newly-filled hot water bottle, satisfied that he had shown us the depth to which he had sunk. He was outdone by Uncle Frank and Auntie Gertie, the discovery of whose illicit goings-on coincided with one of his turns. He was promptly bundled off back to bed to escape moral contagion and, in the general confusion, added to his delirium, showed a commendable grasp of the situation, forgetting to take a hot water bottle and muttering darkly about what sounded like "whores". He recovered completely, being next seen with his woods as a member of the Recreation Bowling Club team for their annual fixture against the local team and in high good humour at having won his 'end'.

We can pass over Uncle George, who had long before emigrated to America where he stayed throughout the period. Although he was not directly involved in the affairs of the family, he was not without influence. He it was who influenced my father to emigrate to the United States and gave shelter to him on his arrival. He continued to represent the family interest in America which was semi-proprietorial and he has always exerted a fascination for the Sigsworth branch. The earliest American forbear of whom I heard was a relative of my grandmother, whom he alarmed on his return, having made his pile, by sitting at her kitchen table with his Colt 45 at the ready in case someone came 'tarryhootin' around. Thank heaven no one came in with a vestige of a tarryhoot about him, or grand Uncle Tom would sure as hell have demonstrated his prowess. He contented himself by outlining plans to build a model pig farm near Selby, with sties done out in white tiling and everything to match. It would inaugurate a new deal for pigs. Nothing came of it except the return of Uncle Tom to the States where he is lost to view.

Great Aunt Sarah is even more obscure. I think she helped when I was born but the rest is silence. I have a small green ornament which belonged

78

to her, otherwise her passage is unmarked. George and his family remained in America. Gertie made two trips, one with the object of staying, but had obviously left it too late and it ended in tears, and the return of an unchastened Gertie. Clearly it was the United States' loss. Apart from a couple of visits which were not a success, after the Second World War ties were weakened. With all the surviving relatives older, more fixed in their ways, and meaner and crabbier, disposed to be patronising to the point of offensiveness if American, or prickly and quick to defend all things British, the visits were foredoomed to failure. This in spite of the almost proprietorial attitude of the British Sigsworths to their American guests. It is true that they had shown little disposition to move from the district in which they had always lived and inhabited the same sort of house, displaying a contentment with their environment which the Americans found hard to understand.

Seen with fresh eyes, New Wortley and Holbeck must have looked unprepossessing dumps. They were. To be renting some of the area's many back-to-back houses was not exactly an indicator of high aspirations. Uncle Herbert, with his wife Alice and their three children, had moved to the opposite side of the road: from the Tilburys to the Eustons, from a back-to-back to a small through-house, one of a small terrace built as in-filling of a triangle of ground in the 1930s. By the time of the American visits he was dead. He had been gassed in the 1914-18 war which left him with stomach ulcers and a high propensity to asthma. When the railway company saw fit to upgrade him from a guard to a station-master, they sent him to Marple which aggravated his asthma to such unbearable levels that he had to resign and go back to being a guard. My main memory is of him fighting for breath like a newly landed fish, and my having shown no sympathy. I blush in retrospect for being so intolerant and cruel. That is all there is to Uncle Herbert's tale.

Imagine the attic of a back-to-back house: a box about ten feet square, cut in half into a wedge shape in accordance with the slope of the roof. In a room of these dimensions my seven maternal uncles slept. Imagine such a room lighted and ventilated by a small skylight. Imagine, further, one of the brothers having from birth an incontinent bladder. Where, incidentally, did they put their clothes? Think of the state of the air in a morning. Remember that as far as personal hygiene was concerned there was one cold water tap between ten people. It was a situation accepted without complaint. My mother, for example, regarded life at home before the family began to break up as a golden age and would not be persuaded otherwise by any talk of overcrowding, poverty, mortality or any gloomier statistics which are part of the stock-in-trade of the social historian.

The attic could only have accommodated a double and one single bed. What miracles of compression dictated the distribution of bodies between them is a mystery which will never be solved, but it must have made for uneasy nights. There were two groups in the family. My grandparents produced Walter, Charles, Harry and Clifford in quick succession, followed after an interval of about ten years by Robert, George, Arthur and my mother. There was another sister who died during my mother's infancy and at least one miscarriage attested to by my mother, who remembered my granny with her skirts pinned up to catch the blood while she did the washing which she had walked to the other side of Leeds to collect. The very idea of the relatively rich in the north of the town graciously doling out their soiled clothes to be washed at sweated rates of pay by women like my grandmother, with only one cold water tap in the house and an absence of other facilities, symbolises what a God-awful society Edwardian England was for the poor or those in any way economically fragile.

Another way in which poverty manifested itself was the humiliation of Charles, who had to wear a pair of girl's button-up boots – the kind that extended over the calf – leaving no doubt about the sex of the wearer. They were probably a pair handed down by one of Grandma's clients for washing and fitted Charley best. He was not grateful. I don't know much about Charley. He had quarrelled bitterly with his parents and, though he lived with his wife, Elsie, just a few doors up the road, he rarely visited them, and his wife never did. The cause of the rift was never referred to, and whenever Charles' or Elsie's name cropped up in conversation it was always in hushed tones, with warning glances in my direction. I always felt obscurely guilty on these occasions, but never did find out what the cause of the quarrel was. During the 1930s Charles was unemployed for a long time, which did nothing to sweeten his disposition, and my memory of when we met is of a bitter man wearing a white muffler.

Charles was the oldest. Then came Walter whom I never met. He lived and worked in Weymouth, which seemed as remote as Outer Mongolia. He made torpedoes and was a skilled engineer but had had the temerity to marry a Weymouth girl, whose rare excursions North provided an ample diet for mimicry of her rich Dorset accent, which accorded ill with the harsh Leeds speech.

Next came Harry, whom I remember as a signalman at the Barlby box on the busy line between York and London. He, o bliss!, had a smallholding and three children, a boy, Billy, and two girls, Grace and Joan, making our annual visit to order a chicken for Christmas a joy. The chickens were specially reared to a monstrous size and cost five shillings [25p]. The cousins were all older than I, all at secondary schools, and I would willingly have died for any one of them, though my sacrifice would have been unheeded by the two girls whose concerns did not include me, which would have added to the melancholy of the occasion. Uncle Harry was almost as remote to me as Walter because his shifts meant that he was usually at work or asleep.

Clifford had started life as an engineer at Greenwood and Batley's but was thrown out of work in the early 1930s. He opened a fish-and-chip shop, and with the help of his wife made a success of it, so that he bought a car – being the only member of the family on either side to do so – and retired to St. Annes on the Lancashire coast. He was still enjoying his hobby of ballroom dancing until his death in the 1980s.

After an interval Robert arrived. Robert was to prove a heavy burden. Having no control over his bladder he was always soaking wet. Because the family could not afford anything else Robert had to rely on old towels, cut up sheets, and anything else of a cast-off nature that was suitable. One result of his disease was that he had virtually no notion that his – happily rare – condition was of great interest to the medical profession, who subjected him to various operations, incidental pain, and left him still wet and several years behind at school. He never did learn to be literate, but nevertheless ran a successful business on his own as a cobbler, with some help from his younger brother, Arthur. Always cheerful, Robert's workshop echoed to the sound of his whistling and he bore his affliction without complaint. Past retirement age, he went with a routine complaint to the Doctor's. The doctor was young and enthusiastic and far more interested in Robert's lifetime's burden than what he was being consulted about. "I can make you dry," he proclaimed. What he actually meant was that after many pokings and proddings to determine the feasibility, Mr X, THE great man for urological surgery, would sweep into the theatre accompanied by a small army of lesser beings to minister to his needs and perform (how pervasively the language of the theatre remains to be applied to surgery!) all the roles of a supporting cast. This happened and Robert was made dry by diverting the flow of urine into a removable bag into which were deposited his faeces also – a sort of ileostomy. He was noticeably more quiet after this, looking preoccupied and remote. He didn't last long.

Next came George, a quiet, humorous man who was a tailor and suffered from stomach ulcers. He had been gassed in the war and his ulcers were the result, though medically it could not be proved, or so the doctors said who formed the panel to determine his case for a pension. He had also been taken prisoner by the Germans who had treated him civilly as a farm worker. No amount of asking questions would get him to say anything more about the war. It was a taboo subject.

Lastly, there was Arthur, who introduced me to the countryside by pathways long built over, even going as far as Malham Cove, one never-to-be-forgotten day. Arthur was the clerk in a solicitor's office and was still required to make quill pens out of hens' feathers, in order to produce old English writing in the preamble to legal documents. They made awful scratching noises but it was very impressive. One felt in the presence of the majesty of the law. A scintilla of this seemed to cling to Arthur. He was my boyhood hero.

So there you have it. Ten uncles. Eleven, if you count Uncle Frank, though he did not count really, not being related by blood and, in any case, his name was not invoked much after the laying on of hands with Gertie. His religious fervour had to find other outlets and he ended up strapped in a wheelchair having to rest content with making lewd suggestions rather than putting them into practice, which he had been doing before being restrained. He was an awful lesson in taking religion too seriously!

The older generation were not followed as a demographic example by their children. Whereas both sets of grandparents had practised no very tight control over their fertility, their children were content with much more limited proof of its existence and lavished upon one child the care which would previously have been diffused among many. What motivated them to limit the size of their families can only be a matter for guesswork. It was a form of behaviour which was widespread. Nearly all of my friends were the product of one-child families. The fact that there were so many of them would seem to point to a readily identifiable cause but I don't remember any mention of the topic so that one is left in the dark about the lemming-like behaviour of potential parents.

81

This plethora of uncles, all of age for military service, makes one reflect on the thoroughness of the call-up process when it came. Only two, out of eleven, from different sides of the family, for certain served, and it is this which explains the absence of discussion of life in the services, rather than a refusal to disinter the uncomfortable past, of which only one member of the family had any experience. Otherwise, the uncles were typical of their class in society, leading unspectacular lives of a sort which can only be described as blameless.

Frank Sigsworth, Eric's father.

CHAPTER 12

Grammar School

The Grammar School was founded in 1552 and had been rebuilt on the edge of Woodhouse Moor in Victorian gothic. Subsequent additions had been made. A classroom wing had been added, a workshop, swimming bath and gymnasium being conspicuous. Less so, tucked away below the rugby pitch reserved for first team games, were squash and fives courts and the modest bungalow inhabited by Sergeant Young and his wife, he being effectively in charge of the school O.T.C. [Officer Training Corps], a sort of handy man about the office and first line of defence for the headmaster against unwanted callers. So far, so good: the school matched Greyfriars, my model culled from weekly readings of the *Magnet*. The school was, declaimed the brochure issued to prospective parents thinking of sending their offspring to be educated there, a Public School. Apart from a few scholarship boys each year the intake was fee-paying. To make them feel at home the minority were referred to as 'scholars'. There the comparison with Greyfriars ended. It was a crushing disappointment. Where were Famous Five and Harry Wharton, where Vernon Smith? One looked in vain for an equivalent of Lord Mauleverer, and the "Owl of the Remove". There was a conspicuous absence at any level of the school of anyone who would translate into the world of Greyfriars with ease. True, the arrival every day of one of the sixth formers in an MG, with a strap around its bonnet, gave a small thrill to my snobbish yearnings as did the delivery of two brothers in a chauffeur-driven Rolls. The social credit derived from this auspicious daily event was dissipated on learning that the father ran a dance hall in one of the less salubrious areas of Leeds.

Nor did the masters, from the Head down, equate with their fictional counterparts. Instead of a saintly classical scholar other-worldly, yet all-knowing, our Headmaster, it seemed to us, was a terrifying figure, who always caught one acting foolishly – pulling a silly face, or halfway through an imitation of a comedian whose act was pretty terrible anyway without imitation. He was not very tall, rather pompous, a scientist and Welsh. He was given to stalking the corridors during lessons wearing his mortarboard, without a gown, which made him look silly, and he was wheeled in in times of potential crisis such as recruiting for the O.T.C. His technique was simple: he surveyed the class, gave a short address on the virtues of the O.T.C. and then asked any boy who did NOT want to join the Corps to put up his hand.

It worked very well: only two boys indicated dissent. One was crippled and the other had parents who had already written indicating their objections to military service.

The rest of us just sat and gave our tacit support to militarism in general. Unthinkingly, we accepted that the purpose of the bayonet with which we were issued was to disembowel the enemy, to which end we hurled ourselves at bales of straw in default of a warm, breathing body, not forgetting to bring the butt up into the putative face to complete the exercise. We were encouraged to utter loud warlike cries in order to strike fear into the heart of the enemy, assuming that the threat to his vital organs was insufficient or (perish the thought) he was not similarly intent on depriving oneself of some essential organ. Exercises of similar unreality were brought together in an ultimate parody on the Field Day, in which the Corps was divided into two halves – Blueland and Redland. One side was required to defend against attack by the other from some readily discernible natural feature of the landscape on a piece of land known as Adel Moor. It was a large tract of land, long since built over, consisting of silver birch trees, rocks and heather. Teachers acted as umpires, popping up to announce that Red or Blue had been wiped out. This invariably set off loud cries of protest but to no avail. Dead was dead.

After the confusion had been resolved, we all paraded on the playing fields to be addressed by a brigadier from the KOYLI [King's Own Yorkshire Light Infantry] depot who complimented us on our battle and threw in his twopenn'orth about what a great life it was in the army. Then we came to the General Salute. This was the moment when, one year, the Commandant's dog decided to enter the scene. A Great Dane as big as a horse, it ambled on just as the trumpeter started to sound the General Salute. Tail wagging majestically, it advanced on the bass drum and peed on it. Only after it had finished did it obey the frantic calls of its master to come to heel. In his civilian capacity as form-master of Upper V he had doubtless become used to acts of disobedience and gestures of defiance to authority.

Upper V was a collection of young gentlemen who had failed to pass School Certificate, either through inability or disinclination. Major Ward faced them like a District Commissioner dealing with a refractory bunch of tribesmen and in this way kept an uneasy peace, largely by a periodic and exemplary flogging delivered dispassionately but effectively. The whole school seemed to depend on the rule of force. The Head dealt out six strokes at a time; the masters also observed the magic of six, as did the prefects, who enjoyed the privilege of administering corporal punishment. Why six should have this significance attached to it, as in the phrase "six of the best", I do not know. Six blows from a cane, especially when delivered by an eighteen-year-old whose enthusiasm was unmitigated by discretion could hurt a lot and it seemed very silly to give this power to a boy. The school, seen retrospectively, was a monstrously archaic institution. At the time, it seemed perfectly natural and I recall no word of criticism of the regime which resounded to the sound of stick on buttock.

Another thing which caused no raising of the eyebrows was the active expression of anti-semitism. There were Jews throughout the school, a few in every form, usually from wealthy families. Quite a few had anglicised their surnames. They were immediately identified as Jews every morning by their exclusion from school prayers. Then, when the school had completed its devotions, the Jewish boys would file in and split off to join their forms. There was no anti-semitism in this, it could be argued, but it left one feeling uncomfortable. It must be remembered that this was during the 1930s when the poison of anti-semitism, rampant in Germany, was just below the apparently smooth surface of British life. I well remember the first sickening introduction of it into my consciousness. It was in a second-form English class and involved a Jewish boy who was normally an inoffensive boy and a model pupil. He must have been talking out of turn. Suddenly, the master flew into a ferocious rage and rushed up to the offender shouting, "You dirty little yid", twisting his arm behind his back and frog-marching his victim to the front of the class, where he administered a sound thrashing before a shocked audience.

The ferocity of the episode and the disproportionate rage which it provoked and the racism it uncovered were impossible to understand by a class of eleven-year-olds. I confess to being still in the dark when thinking about it. There were no repercussions. The same master continued to make fun of the Jewish contingent in the class for not attending school on Saturdays in accordance with observation of their religious practice and derided their other enforced absences such as Yom Kippur, which he always referred to as Young Kipper, not a devasting piece of wit it is true, but always one-sided and difficult to deal with.

For, as a mere boy in an unsympathetic environment, I knew the sense of impotent rage and injustice arising in a different context. It was the same master's whim to have us read aloud in turn, and it came to be mine. I had not read for long when I was commanded to stop: "Sigsworth! We don't take a bath on the grass, we take a Baarth on the Graass!" How the rest of the class laughed and jeered as I sat red-faced, wanting the floor to open up and swallow me and my nasty working-class accent with its flat 'a's. All hail to the correct speakers of the King's English as they enjoyed their baths on the lawn tended by an army of cloned Sigsworths! An institution in which anti-semitism went unchecked and in which corporal punishment was widely and unquestionably used is far below commonly accepted standards in education now. But I am writing of the school as it was over half a century ago when it was dominated by the middle-class values then current.

There were, on the staff, men, who after the end of the war, would probably have stayed on as Fellows of Colleges, in a kinder economic climate, rather than becoming schoolmasters. Who knows what thwarted ambitions were assuaged at the expense of the smarting rumps which offered such a tempting target. Others had been officers during the war and had turned to schoolmastering as a last refuge offering social status for ex-officers, not too incompatible with ideas conceived in the officers' mess and not needing too high an academic standard. The school rated its academic performance largely in terms of successes at Oxford and Cambridge and its magazine contained reports on old Boys, now undergraduates, in a world-weary style with Wodehousian flashes. Other universities might not have existed. The school had the advantage of access to exhibitions endowed by Lady Margaret Hastings, which were closed to all but a number of Yorkshire schools and tenable at Oxford. This enabled the school to maintain a steady flow of scholars to Oxford, larger than would otherwise have been the case. It is a moot point which was more valued, the winning of a place at Oxford or Cambridge, or one's colours as a full member of the First XV, which entitled one to wear a gaudy blazer in silver, navy and yellow stripes. I suspect the latter, and idled away many an hour dreaming of wearing such a garment, realizing that I lacked the talent to be worthy of more than a tenuous place in the Second XV.

Nor was a place at Oxford or Cambridge a realistic prospect. I consistently failed to grasp anything to do with Latin despite the efforts of the master whose thankless task it was to teach me and whose earnestly held belief was that an education in the classics fitted one for any job, and who sought to prevent one's descent into the ranks of the jobless by frequent beating. He kept a selection of canes in his cupboard, bestowing the name "Algy" on his favourite. He had his victims grab the bottom rung of a chair, folded their jackets back so that the extra layer of cloth would not intervene and afford some measure of protection and proceeded with the ritual punishment. No amount of beating could produce a flicker of interest in Messrs Hillard and Botting's doubtless excellent Latin grammar. I remained obdurate and endured the consequent regular beatings stolidly, harbouring no sense of resentment or injustice. My attempts to make sense of Latin were so bad that we reached a tacit agreement on a sliding scale, relating my mangling of a tongue, which he held dear, to the number of strokes which I would receive. I must have ended the year heavily overdrawn. I have often wondered since about this enthusiasm for inflicting corporal punishment by beating the rumps of adolescent boys. Was one lending oneself to the expiation of a lust derived from the raunchier parts of the classics?

Otherwise there is nothing to add. I was neither wildly unhappy nor happy in the school. Its shortcomings had their origins deep in the structure and values of society and were beyond my comprehension.

Eric at Leeds University (back row, extreme right)

86

Epilogue

Perhaps we should note, since these reminiscences do not tell us, that Eric Sigsworth was born, not in Leeds, but in Trimountain, Michigan, during his father's brief attempt to emigrate to the USA, which Eric mentions in Chapter 11, returning to Leeds when Eric was three. Unlike many of his uncles and their contemporaries, whom we met also in Chapter 11, Eric served a spell in the armed forces, in the Fleet Air Arm, during World War Two, before being discharged with T.B., the disease he discusses so graphically in Chapter 10. Perhaps his involvement in the Officer Training Corps at Leeds Grammar School stood him in good stead, despite the antics of disobedient dogs on solemn occasions. After military service Eric took his degree at the University of Leeds, where he also became a research student and, later, a lecturer in economic history.

The topics which Eric chose to concentrate on in these reminiscences reflect some of his interests as a professional historian – housing, medicine, the clothing and wool textile industries and the many details of day to day life with which he wittily embellished his lectures and some of his writing, to the delight of his audience. Those of us who have heard his informal lecture on 'pure finders' (see Chapter 1) will recognise his mischievous interest in the unmentionable aspects of history, including sex and other bodily functions, which permeates this volume. Yet in these reminiscences we also glimpse some of the real and sometimes miserable consequences history has had on our bodily lives.

It is also apparent, from reading these reminiscences, whose side Eric was on, and his own values and beliefs are made clear for us to see, whether or not they are ones we share. While he pokes fun, for example, at overly houseproud women, it is a kindly fun, noting at the same time the drudgery and hard work of everyday existence for many of the people in the world in which he grew up. It would have been tempting as an editor to draw some parallels with contemporary society, which, had he lived to revise the manuscript, Eric might have drawn himself. But, sadly, we cannot be certain that he would have done this, so the parallels must remain undrawn, except in the reader's own mind.

However, Eric Sigsworth's obituarist, Roy Wilkinson[1] wrote that:
> "He was a warm and emotional person who wore his heart on his sleeve professionally, politically and personally. It was natural

[1] *The Guardian*, Feb. 6, 1992

that he became embroiled in issues of housing policy and typical that he should organise the tenants of a crumbling block in Kirkstall to petition the then housing minister, Keith Joseph, when he visited Leeds."

This volume of reminiscences, while speaking of some of the details and ephemera of a particular boy's life in the 1930s, also gives us some clues concerning the roots of a particular kind of social and historical consciousness, a consciousness which comes from the lives of ordinary people in ordinary houses in ordinary streets.

Rosamund Billington
September, 1994

Eric as a young man, in academic dress and in military uniform (Fleet Air Arm).